STRENGTHENING FISCAL DECENTRALIZATION IN NEPAL'S TRANSITION TO FEDERALISM

JULY 2022

ASIAN DEVELOPMENT BANK

© 2022 Asian Development Bank
6 ADB Avenue, Mandaluyong City, 1550 Metro Manila, Philippines
Tel +63 2 8632 4444; Fax +63 2 8636 2444
www.adb.org

Some rights reserved. Published in 2022.

ISBN 978-92-9269-624-5 (print); 978-92-9269-625-2 (electronic); 978-92-9269-626-9 (ebook)
Publication Stock No. TCS220280
DOI: http://dx.doi.org/10.22617/TCS220280

Notes:
In this publication, "$" refers to United States dollars.

Cover design by Editha Creus.

On the cover: A sound fiscal federalism framework empowers subnational governments and supports efficient and effective delivery of public services, which contribute to local economic and human capital development. (All photos by ADB).

CONTENTS

TABLES, FIGURES, AND BOXES

ACKNOWLEDGMENTS

This report was prepared with technical and financial support under the regional technical assistance project RETA: 9387 Strengthening Institutions for Localizing Agenda 2030 for Sustainable Development of the Asian Development Bank (ADB).

Overall coordination and advisory support was provided by Hiranya Mukhopadhyay, chief of the Governance Thematic Group, and Rachana Shrestha, public management specialist, Sustainable Development and Climate Change Department, ADB.

The review involved Cigdem Akin, principal public management economist, Central and West Asia Department, ADB; Hans van Rijn, principal public management specialist, East Asia Department, ADB; Krishna Pathak, senior public management officer, South Asia Department, ADB; Samuel Hill, senior economist, Economic Research and Regional Cooperation Department, ADB; Vidyadhar Mallik, former finance secretary and minister of federal affairs and local governments in Nepal; and Roy Kelly, professor, Sanford School of Public Policy, Duke University.

ABBREVIATIONS

ADB	Asian Development Bank
COVID-19	coronavirus disease
e-GP	e-government procurement
FCGO	Financial Comptroller General Office
FY	fiscal year
GDP	gross domestic product
ICT	information and communications technology
IGFA	intergovernmental fiscal arrangement
IGFM	intergovernmental fiscal management
IGFT	intergovernmental fiscal transfers
LGO	Local Government Operation (Act)
MOF	Ministry of Finance
MOFAGA	Ministry of Federal Affairs and General Administration
MTEF	medium-term expenditure framework
MARS	Municipal Administration and Revenue System
NPC	National Planning Commission
NNRFC	National Natural Resources and Fiscal Commission
OSR	own source revenue
PATA	policy and advisory technical assistance
SNG	subnational government
SuTRA	Subnational Treasury Regulatory Application
TDF	Town Development Fund
VAT	value-added tax

CURRENCY EQUIVALENTS
(as of 8 June 2022)

Currency unit – Nepalese rupees (NRs)
NR1.00 = $0.0080427229
$1.00 = NRs124.336000

The fiscal year (FY) of the Government of Nepal ends on 15 July. "FY" before a calendar year denotes the year in which the fiscal year ends, e.g., FY2020 ends on 15 July 2020.

EXECUTIVE SUMMARY

I. Introduction

This report updates and synthesizes studies of policy and advisory technical assistance (PATA 9150) funded by the Asian Development Bank (ADB) and conducted in support of Nepal's transition to federalism. It notes the progress of regulatory and policy reforms that seek to operationalize an ambitious restructuring of the state, one that embodies a deep commitment to fiscal decentralization. Lessons offered in the report could help the Government of Nepal to adopt and refine a robust fiscal federalism framework. The lessons learned could also be useful to stakeholders contemplating a similar state transition in other countries.

II. Nepal's Fiscal Federalism Framework

Nepal's shift to a federal state structure helped to end a long internal conflict by establishing a unifying and equitable political system. The 2015 Constitution restructures the overall governance structure of the country creating three levels of government: federal, provincial, and local. The Constitution aims for cooperative federalism with substantial fiscal decentralization. It sets out the functions of each level (and concurrent functions) in its schedules. Legislative elaboration and implementation of federalism are well advanced, although some aspects remain works in progress.

Much work remains to be done on the four main components of fiscal decentralization: (i) assignment of expenditure functions and the budgeting process; (ii) revenue mobilization; (iii) intergovernmental transfers; and (iv) subnational borrowing. Stressing fiscal decentralization makes it clear that the Nepal state wishes to empower subnational governments (SNGs) giving them more discretion and autonomy, while at the same time ensuring greater accountability in the operation of these newly empowered governments.

The report examines progress on the four elements of fiscal decentralization (covering the constitutional and legislative framework, implementation, reform efforts, and recommendations), returning frequently to the themes of discretion and accountability .

III. Public Expenditure Assignment and Budgeting

Constitutional and Legislative Framework. A key institution established in the new constitution is the National Natural Resources and Fiscal Commission (NNRFC). It sets guidelines for federal fiscal transfers to SNGs and formulas for distributing natural resource royalties. With these resources, each level of government is empowered to plan and budget, in principle, according to the functions assigned to it. Making this challenging is the high degree of concurrence in the Constitution.

The government has sought to clarify expenditure assignments by unbundling the schedules of the Constitution in laws on a subnational level and other legal instruments; over 1,000 government functions have been detailed. This disaggregation has only been partly helpful to SNGs. Concurrence still hampers action and the connection between the expenditure functions and the finances remains murky.

Progress in elaborating public expenditure management is evident at all levels of government, governing financial procedures and seeking to give spending a strategic character.

Implementation. The legislative framework for structuring and guiding SNGs has largely been set and is being applied by SNGs to the extent that their emerging capacities allow. The new budgeting cycle at the provincial level began in 2018. The actual spending patterns of SNGs are being tracked through a new accounting and treasury package, the Subnational Treasury Regulatory Application (SuTRA). The rollout is not yet complete, and it is hard to tell as of 2021 whether the federal government will be able to track expenditures on the basis of both the general economic functions and the specific functions assigned to provinces and local government.

Available data suggest that SNG spending in total is growing (to 36% of total expenditures as of 2020) but is not sufficiently offset by a reduction in national government spending, generating some pressure on the government debt. While spending levels are heading in the right direction, SNGs face challenges in absorbing allocations due to capacity limitations and the disruptive influence and response to the coronavirus disease (COVID-19) pandemic.

Due to the early stage of data system development and analysis, it is not possible to say whether expenditure patterns since 2018 (when provincial budgets first were put in place) reflect the constitutionally desired equalization effect of federal or provincial grants. The data does show that some provinces are getting more grants than others, but the story of how this links to revenue capacity and overall equity has yet to emerge.

Reforms. The Government of Nepal has taken concrete measures to improve public financial management at all levels. It has provided SNGs with:

(i)   guidance on organizational structures,
(ii)   guidelines on annual budgeting and medium-term expenditure framework (MTEF) approaches,
(iii)   support for establishing an e-government procurement (e-GP) system,
(iv)   support in the use of the SuTRA, and
(v)   Support for an information and communications technology (ICT)-based online Nepal audit management system.

The pace of these changes has been brisk, stretching limited capacities at the subnational level (e.g., in the application of the MTEF). It has also tested the vertical coordination and support linkages within the federal government and revealed challenges of horizontal coordination across federal agencies in guiding SNGs.

Service delivery at the subnational level has been hampered by uncertainties about who is responsible for service functions. The ad hoc approach to the COVID-19 response confirms this. The lack of clarity on service-level obligations (their obligatory nature and standards of performance) further weakens service delivery by denying it appropriate vertical accountability. SNG internal audit mechanisms are still under development. Mechanisms for holding SNGs accountable to citizens also need to be strengthened.

Recommendations. A prioritized approach to unfinished framework elaboration and additional reforms are needed, with the pace reflecting SNG capacity as this develops. Efforts that promise to achieve greater discretion for SNGs while increasing their accountability include the following:

(i)   Greater clarity in functions assigned to SNGs, including how these will be financed. This clarification should work to resolve unhelpful concurrence.

(ii)   Setting performance expectations for subnational expenditure and the mechanisms through which these will be incentivized or sanctioned.

(iii)   Orienting budgeting to be more outcome-oriented, particularly for those functions that have stringent performance expectations.

(iv)   Enhancing intergovernmental coordination to ensure that federal and SNGs are focusing on their respective functions and that there is avoidance of duplication (unless concurrence is intended and intergovernmental action is interlocking and coordinated).

(v)   Reviewing and amending laws and regulations (largely pre-federal) that contradict the new assignment of functions as set in the Constitution and its related legislation. Harmonization may be needed in some instances, making use of the results of the unbundling exercise where these elaborated lists find consensus.

(vi)   Informing the public about the new responsibilities of the government and facilitating the application of the social accountability movement in Nepal to focus on making SNGs accountable for their new functions.

(vii)   Enhancing the internal audit system in provinces and local governments where these are inadequate.

IV.   Revenue Mobilization

Constitutional and Legislative Framework. Nepal's new intergovernmental system creates a large vertical fiscal gap; 85% of revenues flow to the federal government, whereas most public services are delivered by SNGs. Hence, SNG revenues fall far short of meeting expenditure needs. This feature is not self-correcting as federal government taxes (such as value-added tax—VAT— or customs) are more buoyant than taxes of SNGs.

The vertical fiscal gap is addressed in part by sharing revenues, but the bulk of revenues remain with the federal government.

Non-tax revenues of SNGs for services fall under the jurisdictions of the responsible level of government and are in principle tied to defraying the cost of services.

Implementation. Government revenue increased to 22% of gross domestic product during 2010–2020. That compares well with similar countries but is still insufficient to ensure that expenditure functions assigned to SNGs are well funded. The COVID-19 pandemic slowed revenue growth in 2020–2021, especially in tourism. Moreover, some new SNG taxes are difficult to collect (e.g., the provincial agriculture tax).

Efforts have been made by the government to clarify the substantial concurrence in revenue assignment (especially between provincial and local governments). This has not dispelled all disagreement on the interpretation of statutes or guidance.

Local governments have launched initiatives to increase revenues, making use of their new powers. Some of these have been successful, such as city efforts to accurately record local businesses to determine tax liability more accurately. Large differences in revenue generation exist horizontally (between same level SNGs) reflecting different capacities to undertake tax collection, clean up tax arrears, curb corrupt practices, and upgrade the skills of tax officials. Some of these capacity differences can be overcome by local efforts and support from higher levels of government. Ultimately, equalizing grants will be needed to close the remaining gaps. Local governments rely on grants of 78% to form their budgets.

Reforms. The Government of Nepal is seeking to improve provincial and local government revenue potential and administration. It has adjusted some taxes (vehicle, agricultural income, entertainment, and advertising) to facilitate the collection of the taxes and to set the sharing between SNG levels. Improvements in revenue mobilization will depend on the political reforms undertaken by SNGs to increase taxpayer numbers and compliance. For instance, countering the SNG tendency to opt for more politically expedient approaches (e.g., avoiding implementing the agricultural income taxes).

Recommendations. Local revenue mobilization depends on the clarity of revenue assignment, i.e., which level gets to set, collect, and share various taxes (revenue rights). Moreover, local tax efforts are supported by citizens who can hold SNGs to account for the taxes and fees charged. Improvements are warranted on the following:

(i) Reviewing and amending laws and policies to ensure clarity and consistency in the demarcation of revenue rights of SNGs.

(ii) Assisting SNGs to improve their own source revenue (OSR) by encouraging

    (a) the linkage of revenues to expenditures to promote efficiency, transparency, and accountability;

    (b) pro-business policies at the local level to grow the sources of revenue;

    (c) digitization of transactions and taxation systems; and

    (d) establishing taxpayer awareness campaigns and grievance redressal mechanisms to ensure fairness and willingness to pay.

(iii) Developing new sources of revenue for SNGs by attaching them to federal taxes or finding other sources such as carbon and pollution tax. This effort should follow maximizing revenue sources already assigned.

V. Intergovernmental Fiscal Transfers

Constitutional and Legislative Framework. Intergovernmental grants play a large role in Nepal due to the vertical fiscal gap created by expenditure and revenue assignment. The National Natural Resources and Fiscal Commission Act (2017), Intergovernmental Fiscal Management Act (2017), and Local Level Operation Act (2017) provide the legal framework for fiscal transfers, defining the transfers and distribution criteria for grants and revenue sharing. Provincial and local governments receive four types of grants: fiscal equalization, conditional, special, and matching.

Provincial governments are also mandated to transfer funds to local governments, but their role is heavily constrained by the National Natural Resources and Fiscal Commission (NNRFC). The federal government appears to treat both the provinces and the local governments as essentially similar—as levels of SNGs that are financially subordinate to the federal government—supplying both levels with substantial grants.

Revenue sharing (in addition to the grant system) is predictable, mandated as a proportion of revenue intake, with the federal government retaining the bulk (e.g., 70% of VAT and custom excise taxes) and the rest shared between provincial and local governments (e.g., 15% each for VAT and excise taxes).

Implementation. Revenue sharing and grants have grown slowly. Conditional grants have been the most dominant of the four grant types for local government, whereas the expectation had been that fiscal equalization grants would be the key grants to close the gap between expenditure needs and revenue potential. Moreover, the degree of equity built into the distribution formula of fiscal equalization grants is questioned by some SNGs, such as whether it corresponds with the Constitution's intent

(Article 60[2]). Equalization grants are not predictable in the sense that they are not tied to national revenue intake.

At the local government level, the strong shift to conditional grants suggests that the federal government is seeking to strongly direct local government spending (as opposed to using a large block equalization grant, output, or outcome standards, or allowing the province to shape grants to local governments). The shift away from fiscal equalization grants raises the question of whether the provinces and local governments are being treated equitably.

Provincial transfers to local governments have been much smaller than those transferred by the federal government; federal transfers to local governments in FY2021 were about 10 times larger than those provided by the provincial governments.

Performance-based grants—an experiment dating back two decades—have yet to be incorporated into the equalization grant in a significant way. The government intends to expand its role and enlarge the scope from rewarding governance processes to achievement in service delivery. An expansion in the role of these grants could come at the cost of pursuing equity considerations in resources for development and services across SNGs. Performance grants may best be incorporated into other types of grants and should probably not be prematurely introduced when the system is still seeking to attain basic compliance with main grants.

Recommendations. Efforts to improve the intergovernmental grant system will need to consider the multiple purposes and tensions within these. Some productive directions could include the following:

(i)   Increasing the share of performance-based transfers in a way that does not undermine horizontal equity (where all citizens obtain similar service

provision), prioritizing incentives for SNG revenue mobilization.

(ii)   Anchoring annual grant allocations for SNGs in legislation to promote certainty and accountability.

(iii)   Determining a minimum fixed portion of all revenue collected by the federal government to be transferred to the provinces and local governments to give more predictability and stability to grants.

VI. Subnational Borrowing

Constitutional and Legislative Framework. The Constitution permits all three levels of government to borrow funds to meet expenditure needs that cannot be met through regular resources. Provincial and local governments may borrow domestically, subject to approval from the federal government.

Legislation also allows provincial governments to issue bonds (debentures) but excludes local governments from these powers.

Implementation. While state policy on SNG borrowing is permissive, the regulatory framework is still being developed. Hence, borrowing at the subnational level remains very low in contrast to the strong private sector growth in credit seen in recent years. The NNRFC has set limits annually for SNG borrowing, but these are disconnected from the actual potential for borrowing as of 2021. SNG borrowing—derived largely from state banks—comprises only 0.85% of total local (municipal) revenues.

There is a lack of a strong domestic capital market, and there are not many institutions that serve the municipal credit segment except for the Town Development Fund (TDF). The restructuring of the TDF promises to be supportive of a municipal capital market. The revamped TDF will be renamed and will serve both provincial and municipal governments. It will continue to mobilize domestic and foreign assistance to channel financing to SNGs but will expand its sources of financing, including capital markets.

SNGs have yet to issue debentures, reflecting a capital market environment where even corporate bonds are uncommon. The market is exceedingly thin in both supply and demand. Clarifying the access of local government to bond issuing may require legislative changes. These could serve to introduce conditions to qualify SNGs while maintaining a cautious approach.

Recommendations. Building on the generally permissive framework for SNG borrowing, Nepal can improve access and cautious debt management by the following:

(i) Clarifying guidelines and institutional requirements. In particular, the mandate for issuing debentures and bonds by local governments needs to be explicitly codified in law. National guidelines for SNGs on managing debt need to be provided, and the SNGs will need to develop their policies and debt managing units to adhere to the national framework. New or more suitable organizational units— particularly at the provincial level— should be established for effective debt management, e.g., a debt management office.

(ii) Working on the supply side of lending. This will require making the private banking sector more familiar with SNGs and expanding the reach of financial intermediaries like the TDF. A suggested approach is the creation of desk offices of the TDF for each of the seven provinces. This would allow the TDF to better respond to SNG requests for project-based capital financing. Further reforms include the creation

of provincial-level TDFs following the framework of the federal model.

(iii) Tracking SNG debt at the national level to ensure there will be transparency and macroeconomic vigilance. An important way to work toward this vigilance will be to expand the use of the debt operations and management system to include domestic borrowings by SNGs. This would allow for better management of public debt and would lead to a "single source of truth" concerning public debt of the various tiers of government in Nepal.

VII. Conclusions and Lessons from Nepal's Journey toward Fiscal Federalism

Several conclusions can be drawn from the efforts of Nepal to embrace fiscal federalism:

(i) Nepal is making headway in its efforts to establish a decentralized form of federalism. It has much further to go to empower SNGs in line with the Constitution's intent.

(ii) Because the reform agenda is vast, 5 years is insufficient to see it fully implemented, particularly as the COVID-19 pandemic has acted as a brake. Both the federal government and SNGs are feeling the effect of reform overload.

(iii) Robust reforms call for persistent efforts to assess and develop the capacity of key actors in reform design and implementation; development partners can continue to play a useful role in this effort.

(iv) Reform design and refinement of practice require multistakeholder platforms that can be used to prioritize, sequence, and assess the implementation of reforms. These platforms are new in Nepal and must be supported to give room for the following to vent their grievances and offer suggestions; a bottom–up view that is critical to finding workable solutions.

The experiences of Nepal in shifting from a centralized unitary state structure to a decentralized federal structure provide useful lessons for the refinement of that system and for stakeholders in other countries wishing to undertake the same journey. These lessons include the following:

(i)   It takes time to bring about new policies, legal frameworks, and practices. Time is needed to change mindsets, and broad stakeholder support must be maintained.

(ii)   A reform road map—embedded in a communication strategy—is needed from the start to manage a deep set of political and administrative reforms.

(iii)   It is important to show some initial success on issues that matter to citizens to maintain support and momentum for reforms. This approach calls for phased reforms that do not overwhelm the capacities of key actors.

(iv)   Pursuing fiscal decentralization means ensuring that there is sufficient discretion given to SNGs; in legislation that accords with the constitutional provisions, and capacity development that allows SNGs to make full use of their new powers.

(v)   As SNGs are given more resources and discretion, it becomes more important to hold SNGs accountable. This means that intergovernmental roles and assigned functions need to be well demarcated to enable citizens to know who is responsible, that concurrence is purposeful, and that its operational mechanism is well understood.

(vi)   A federal system that gives both discretion and accountability means bringing stakeholders together to give it shape and making refinements as lessons of implementation emerge. Coordination mechanisms that are workable and trusted are essential to maintain the goodwill of key stakeholders as they work together to shape their relationships in a process that respects their distinct and interdependent roles.

CHAPTER I

INTRODUCTION

This report provides a synthesis and update of previous individual studies conducted by the policy and advisory technical assistance (PATA 9150) funded by the Asian Development Bank (ADB) and successfully concluded in 2018.[1] It draws from fieldwork and engagement with Government of Nepal officials to make observations on the progress of policy and regulatory reforms that seek to operationalize an ambitious restructuring of the state, from a unitary form to a federation that is marked by the devolution of power and resources. While the reforms are happening as part of a broad political restructuring to federalism, this report focuses on the fiscal decentralization that is expected to characterize intergovernmental relationships. Nepal has taken concrete steps since the introduction of the 2015 Constitution to shape its intergovernmental relations to reflect good practices in fiscal decentralization. The report seeks to capture this progress, highlight reforms still needed, and draw lessons that can further assist the Government of Nepal to bring about a robust fiscal decentralization framework.

This report also serves policymakers and stakeholders in other countries who are transitioning to federalism or contemplating such a move. More broadly, it can inform efforts toward fiscal decentralization in unitary or federal countries; such efforts may be more common than wholesale transitions from unitary to federal state structures.

The Report at a Glance

The Government of Nepal—with the support of ADB—prepared the PATA report in 2018. The main objective of the report was to understand the government systems and to develop a fiscal decentralization framework in line with the newly formulated Constitution of Nepal. It also provided crucial policy recommendations to operationalize the suggested framework.

Following the PATA recommendations, significant steps have been taken by the Government of Nepal to implement the framework. As may be expected in such a comprehensive and deep set of reforms, multiple challenges have been faced at the federal and subnational government (SNG) levels. This report highlights the high-level guidance (the Constitution or legislation) in place and the efforts to shape operational instruments and mechanisms to develop and facilitate the implementation of the fiscal federalism framework. This report updates the recommendations of the earlier technical assistance efforts that are still relevant today, and

---

[1]   ADB. 2019. *Technical Completion Report (TA 9150) Nepal: Strengthening Subnational Public Management.* Manila.

that may be relevant to other countries going through or contemplating a similar transition.

This report begins with an overview of the institutional arrangements in Nepal for achieving the objectives of fiscal federalism (Chapter II). The centrality of achieving greater devolution through these new arrangements warrants the application of a fiscal decentralization framework for Nepal, one that links the fiscal components to the broader themes of SNG discretion, local service delivery, and accountability.[2] The framework is explained and guides the analysis in subsequent chapters.

In Chapters III–VI, the study covers the constitutional expectations and early implementation of each of the components of fiscal decentralization. Each of these chapters is structured into constitutional and legislative mandates, findings on the implementation of these mandates (including ongoing initiatives and reforms), challenges faced in making progress on reforms, and recommendations to further cohere elaboration and implementation of that component of the fiscal decentralization framework.

Some conclusions and lessons pertain to the experience of Nepal in forging and implementing a federal system that has a core commitment to the realization of fiscal decentralization, which calls for careful attention to the issues of discretion and accountability of SNGs (Chapter VII). The study notes the approaches called for to ensure that capacity exists at all government levels for the ongoing refinement of a system that works based on respect for constitutionally enshrined intergovernmental roles and the unavoidable interdependence.

Limitations

The report draws its content largely from the period of work of ADB technical assistance (2016–2018), with some updates where data and views could be obtained during 2019 and mid-2021. This was a difficult time for Nepal —as in most other countries—given the coronavirus disease (COVID-19) pandemic. This limited the possibility of close engagement with the government whose priorities were directed to managing the crisis. Moreover, the transition to new fiscal arrangements has taken some time, limiting the number of budget cycles with new arrangements in place. Combined with the impact on revenues and expenditures due to the pandemic, observations and conclusions based on the spending patterns that emerge need to be treated with caution. A longer time frame will be needed to see how the actual components of fiscal decentralization play out with constitutional provisions.

---

[2]   The term "subnational government" (SNG) is used in this report to refer to both or either provincial and local governments. The specific level is otherwise mentioned.

CHAPTER II

INSTITUTIONAL ARRANGEMENTS FOR ACHIEVING THE OBJECTIVES OF FISCAL FEDERALISM IN NEPAL

Background

Nepal is a landlocked Himalayan country in South Asia that is emerging from decades of internal conflict by embracing a political solution that places federalism as its core unifying feature. It is one of the world's poorest countries, with poverty aggravated by the COVID-19 pandemic that according to a UNICEF study has placed more than half of Nepalese households at risk of falling back into poverty because of loss of jobs and income. Gross domestic product (GDP) per capita had just crossed $1,000 in fiscal year (FY) 2018.

Despite its many years of internal conflict, Nepal has in recent years (2016–2020) made considerable progress in its economic growth (Table 1) and its journey toward a more inclusive democracy. It shed monarchical rule, abated violent internal conflict, and attained a measure of economic stability. Political negotiations over a decade to end internal strife culminated in the 2015 Constitution declaring Nepal a federal democratic republic with a commitment to integrating ethnic and political groups into a more just society.

One of the most important changes in the shift to a three-tiered federal system of governance has been the state restructuring. Before this change, the SNG was composed of districts, municipalities, and villages. The central government used to reach down to the local level through its regional branches and certain key positions embedded in district offices. Under the state restructuring, many villages were amalgamated into larger local governments. The districts now have indirect local democratic representation but have in practice become platforms for central government management.

The regional branches of the central government have been largely absorbed by the new level of the province. The restructured SNG is elected democratically and comprises 7 provinces and 753 local governments. While each tier has legislative and executive functions and authority, local governments have judicial functions too, under exclusive and shared jurisdictions. All these changes have required new institutional arrangements for staffing, funds flow, and coordination.

The assignment of expenditure functions shows a high degree of concurrence, where the federal level is expected to exert legislative leadership (Appendix 1). It can also be noted that residual functions (those not listed in the constitutional schedules that may arise in the future) are assigned to the federal government. The federal government also maintains considerable influence over local government, unlike many federal nations with advanced economies where the formative units are given a larger role in shaping local government frameworks.

Table 1: Nepal at a Glance

Population and Geography	Economic and Social Data
Area: 147,180 km²	GDP: $ 34.5 billion (2020)
Population: 29.3 million (2017)	GDP per capita: 1,196 (2020)
Density: 199 inhabitants/km²	Real GDP growth: 7.5% (2017)
Urban population: 19.3 % of national population	Unemployment rate: 2.7% (2017)
Capital city: Kathmandu (4.5% of national population)	Public debt: 36.4% of GDP (2020)
	Human Dev Index: 0.602 (medium) (2020)

Source: World Observatory on Subnational Government Finance and Investment. 2021[3]; World Bank. 2021. Nepal Development Update.

A strong central role is also favored by the constitutional commitment to providing citizens with equal access to services and prioritizing remote or lagging regions (Constitution Article 51.h). These constitutional features suggest that the federation will find a proper balance between the federation and its formative units only if it truly realizes the intergovernmental relations principles of cooperation, coexistence, and coordination (Article 232.1). Because of the unitary history of Nepal—and the general provisions of the Constitution—a great deal of devolution will need to be manifested in its elaboration of the laws, regulations, and policies of the state to realize the spirit of the Constitution.

State policies embedded in the Constitution require SNGs to be participatory and to exhibit good governance. The Constitution requires that state, provincial, and—especially—local government must ensure equal and easy access of citizens to the services and facilities delivered by the state while making public administration fair, free from corruption, and accountable. This is a huge expectation as SNGs have struggled to deliver on similar promises in the past, and the new administrations of the provinces are still taking shape as of 2021.

The legislative and institutional framework for developing the new intergovernmental relations is still a work in progress. The state restructuring has created national level institutions to realize the constitutional intent. For instance, the National Natural Resource and Fiscal Commission (NNRFC) was established to ensure equitable distribution of revenue from natural and financial resources across SNGs. This constitutional body plays an important role given the fiscal gap (vertical fiscal imbalance) at provincial and local levels as they seek to deliver the mandated services in the face of rather limited revenue potential in comparison with that of the federal government.

Some national organizations maintained their names but now operate according to new or amended legislation that recognizes the federal nature of the state (e.g., the Ministry of Federal Affairs and General Administration). Organizational structures and fiscal arrangements have been set in respective legislations (e.g., NNRFC Act, Local Government Operation (LGO) Act). The Civil Servant Adjustment Act was passed in February 2019 to allow for the provisional appointment of key civil service posts while the more comprehensive civil service law governing all civil servants is being prepared. Many other legal instruments related to fiscal matters have been prepared or are under preparation.

---

[3]   World Observatory on Subnational Government Finance and Investment. https://www.sng-wofi.org/country-profiles/Fiche%20NEPAL.pdf (accessed 17 August 2021).

The National Planning Commission (NPC) continues to guide development policy, periodic plans, and sector policies, but must now be even more mindful of the new assignment of functions across levels of government. Under the Ministry of Finance (MOF), a new division dedicated to managing coordination for intergovernmental fiscal management among the tiers of government has been created.

The restructured and slightly renamed Ministry of Federal Affairs and General Administration (MOFAGA) has the role of coordination, cooperation, facilitation, and monitoring and evaluation of activities undertaken by local governments. It also regulates the civil service in the country at all levels. A crucial role for MOFAGA is ensuring that local governments receive the capacity development support needed to manage the new institutional arrangements of federalism. These national organizations are guided in their roles by the relatively new LGO Act, 2017 (2074) and the Intergovernmental Fiscal Arrangement Act, 2017 (2074). These two acts address the revenue rights, revenue sharing, grants, loans, budget arrangements, and public expenditure arrangements of SNGs.

Development partners are supporting Nepal's transition to federalism; ADB provided specific support to several components of fiscal federalism and decentralization. Implementing the shift to federalism in Nepal presents many challenges. Few low-income countries have attempted such comprehensive state restructuring. The administrative capacities of provincial and local governments to deliver and manage services are not yet well developed, and the federal government has only managed an intergovernmental system that was centralized and not very effective.

Much has been accomplished during 2015–2021, but the legislative framework is not yet complete. Stakeholders are not yet familiar with their new powers and responsibilities. Moreover, there has not been a comprehensive implementation plan or a timetable for sequencing the introduction of new policies.[4] Development partners have in many cases cooperated in providing capacity development support to all levels of government. Support has come in the form of policy-based lending to incentivize reforms, and technical assistance to undertake analytical exercises (e.g., public expenditure assessments) and training for new SNG roles.

In examining the emergence of Nepal's fiscal system, it is appropriate to use a fiscal decentralization framework. The terms "fiscal federalism" and "fiscal decentralization" are often used interchangeably. But it is worth stressing—in the case of Nepal—that what is in play is fiscal decentralization, a term that underlines the sharing of power to collect or receive revenues and spend with a certain level of discretion within acknowledged subject areas (functions).

The federation created in Nepal came not from separate entities coming together (and yielding some powers to the federal level), but from a heavily centralized unitary state that sought to keep its diverse regions together by attaining a new social and political compact that entails the devolution of expenditure and revenue powers to the elected SNGs. While in practice investigations of fiscal federalism and fiscal decentralization cover similar ground— i.e., the four components shown in Figure 1— placing stress on fiscal decentralization makes it clear that the intent is to empower SNGs, giving them more discretion and autonomy

---

4   Georgia State University, Andrew Young School of Public Policy, and the Nepal Administrative Staff College. 2019. *Capacity Needs Assessment for the Transition to Federalism.* Sponsored by the Government of Nepal, Ministry of Federal Affairs and General Administration, World Bank Group, and United Nations Development Programme.

while at the same time ensuring greater accountability.[5]

A high degree of autonomy allows SNGs to be proactive, mobilize resources, and shape solutions that fit their circumstances. They will be more vested in searching for efficient solutions to service delivery challenges. A high level of accountability keeps the government responsive to citizens, open about how it functions and performs, and eager to do better. The accountability applies in both directions: to the federal government (and more broadly the state) and citizens located under the SNGs.

The understanding of fiscal decentralization calls for an examination of the four elements in Figure 1 in terms of how they contribute to the high-level objectives of increasing discretion and accountability. This report seeks to align the discussion of the four elements of fiscal decentralization to these themes of discretion and accountability.

Figure 1: Fiscal Decentralization Framework

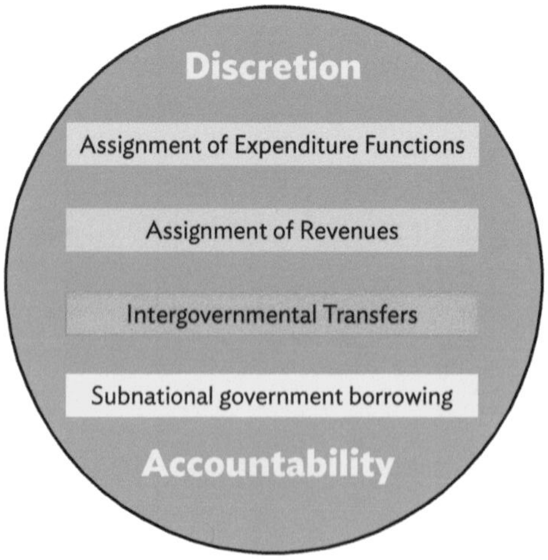

Source: S. Yilmaz et al. 2010. Linking Local Government Discretion and Accountability in Decentralisation. *Development Policy Review*. https://papers.ssrn.com/sol3/papers.cfm?abstract_id=1583149.

---

5   S. Yilmaz et al. 2010. How to Note : A Framework for the Assessment of Fiscal Decentralization System. *Social Development Notes*; No. 123. Washington, DC: World Bank.

CHAPTER III

PUBLIC EXPENDITURE ASSIGNMENT AND BUDGETING

Constitutional and Legislative Framework

Nepal's federal structure calls for planning and budgeting at federal, provincial, and local government levels that match the scope of their assigned functions as listed in the Constitution. One of the main pillars of effective fiscal decentralization is the assignment of expenditure to SNGs. The federal character comes through in the specification of the functions for each level of government enshrined in the Constitution of Nepal (Schedules 5–9). The centralized nature of the federation is evident in the "residual" set of functions being assigned to the federal government.

Each level is empowered to "enact law, make annual budget, take necessary decisions, formulate policies and plans, and implement them in regard to the subjects related to the fiscal power under their jurisdictions." Achieving this match between the legal assignment and development practice depends on the clarity given in the assignment of functions.

Concurrent expenditure assignment is a significant feature of the constitutional lists of functions. Concurrence between functions held by the three levels of government arises in the list of "exclusive" functions of the federal,

provincial, or local levels. For instance, Schedule 6 (provincial) and Schedule 8 (local) both mention health, with only a minor difference in phrasing that cannot serve to differentiate them. In describing these government-specific dedicated lists, the Constitution does not use the term "exclusive," making it unclear whether the overlap in these lists was accidental or intentional.

The concurrence also arises in the existence of schedules that explicitly identify certain functions as being held by multiple levels of government (Schedule 7, for federal and provincial, and Schedule 9 for federal, provincial, and local). Many of these formally concurrent functions pertain to basic services (health, education), natural resources, and the environment. The Constitution does not explain how these are to be shared between two or more levels of government. As most basic services will be delivered by the local or provincial levels, clarity on their respective roles is essential. Appendix 1 captures the separate and concurrent lists of these two SNG levels to reveal the degree of intended or unintended concurrence.

To make the expenditure assignment clearer and more operational, the Government of Nepal has unbundled the functions in the constitutional lists. The unbundling work was led by the chief secretary of the government (Office of the

Prime Minister and Council of Ministers). The exercise—departing from the constitutional schedules—generated a federal list of 606 functions, a provincial list of 267 functions, and a local government list of 302 functions.[6] The authors of the report explain that they used "universally acclaimed principles" in elaborating on the constitutional lists, but the report does not show how these were applied.[7] Complicating this picture is the issuance of the Local Government Operation (LGO) Act, 2017 which also has a list of local government functions. It is not clear if this list accords with the unbundled constitutional list. The legal standing of the unbundled list is also unclear (Box 1).

BOX 1
What Is the Status of the Unbundled List?

The chief secretary's report with the unbundled list of functions was approved by Cabinet in 2017, but its legal status is not clear, particularly with prior sector legislation and the Local Government Operation (LGO) Act, 2017. The content has some shortcomings in terms of clearly demarcating functions across levels of government, but the main challenge is to determine how this more detailed list of functions translates into sector and service-specific legal products that can also explain how the different levels relate to each other in discharging the functions (e.g., coordination, conflict and interpretation resolution, financing).

Source: Government of Nepal. 2017. *Unbundling of the Functions of the Federal, Provincial, and Local Levels as per the constitutional annexes* (in original language). Kathmandu.

The Government of Nepal is required by the Constitution to distribute fiscal equalization grants to provincial and local governments based on their expenditure needs and capacity in generating revenue. This constitutional requirement (Article 60.4) makes it important for the government to develop a sound expenditure and revenue data and reporting

BOX 2
Ensuring a Strong Role for Subnational Governments through an Agreed Sharing of Revenues: The Case of Indonesia

Indonesian subnational governments (SNGs) comprise provinces, districts or cities, and villages. Decentralization reforms in 1999 and subsequent amendments have given SNGs important spending responsibilities. However, major sources of revenue remain highly centralized. SNGs accounted for 47.7% of public expenditure in 2016, but only 10.9% of total public revenues. To ensure that SNGs have sufficient funding for the functions assigned to them, the legislation establishes that SNGs will receive at least 26% of net domestic revenue (for a general block grant) and 20% of the Revenue-Sharing Fund from natural resources and other sources (e.g., property tax).

Source: World Observatory on Subnational Government Finance and Investment (accessed 17 August 2021).

system. The Constitution avoids setting any obligatory level of transfers to SNGs based on national revenues as is done in some countries (Box 2). However, revenue sharing that is fixed in its proportions across levels of government is achieved through legislation for some revenue sources (VAT and internal excise, para. 40).

The Constitution calls for the prioritization of poor and underdeveloped regions but seems to also direct the state to ensure that natural resources benefit local people. State development policies (Article 50) direct the state to prioritize poor and underdeveloped regions, suggesting an equalizing role in expenditure management. At the same time, other provisions may cause tension, as natural

---

[6]   Government of Nepal. 2017. *Unbundling of the Functions of the Federal, Provincial, and Local Levels as per the Constitutional Annexes* (in original language). Kathmandu.
[7]   The report lists these as "subsidiarity, economies of scale, efficiency, economic stability, social inclusion and national priority, externalities or spillover jurisdiction, accountability and viability, among others."

resources are to be fairly distributed by giving "local people the priority and preferential rights," suggesting that derivation of natural resources will be a consideration in returning benefits to the SNGs endowed with natural resources. In either case, these considerations suggest that the federal government will play a strong role in expenditure management in the new federation.

A comprehensive legislative and regulatory framework for public expenditure management across all levels of government is emerging. All three levels of government have created legal frameworks to make the constitutional provisions on expenditure roles operational. The legal instruments are numerous and cover approaches to allocations and internal public financial management procedures (e.g., procurement). Some are directed to the national institutions, indicating new or updated procedures. For example, the Financial Procedure and Fiscal Accountability (FPFA) Act, 2019 (2076) institutionalizes financial discipline and lays down well-defined procedures for public sector budgeting.

Other acts are dedicated to SNGs. Notable among these are the Provincial Government Business Rules, 2017 (20740, and the LGO Act, 2017). These two acts outline detailed provisions on the functions of the provincial and local governments in the sectors that fall within their jurisdiction. The arrangements for intergovernmental fiscal transfers are laid out in the Inter-Governmental Fiscal Arrangement Act, 2017 (2074). The Province Financial Procedure **Act**, 2017 (2074), amended 2019 (2076), delves into financial procedures related to the operation and management of the provincial consolidated fund and other government funds; sets out the approach to a medium-term expenditure framework (MTEF); and establishes auditing procedures and budgeting processes. Financial procedures for local governments are set out in the LGO Act, 2017.

Implementation Findings Related to Subnational Government Expenditures and Budgeting

A comprehensive intergovernmental financial data system is being put in place but has yet to be fully implemented, making it difficult to discern whether SNGs are spending under assigned functions. The government made the subnational treasury regulatory application (SuTRA) mandatory—starting FY2020—for the local levels for planning, budgeting, accounting, and reporting. Compliance only began in FY2021. As of 2021, reporting on government expenditures has been done by provinces based on recurrent and capital categories (Appendix 2) and main socioeconomic functions that are similar to the international Classification of the Functions of Government.

Table 2 provides a classification of the functions of government summaries for FY2021, showing that spending is concentrated on economic affairs, public services, and housing and community services. The pattern generally holds across provinces. This level of aggregation obscures whether provinces are fulfilling their assigned functions. At the local level, reporting is even more aggregated and is not yet flowing through the SuTRA system in a way to allow disaggregation by general expenditure functions or the specifics of the constitutional functional assignment. Other sources of data can be used to get a partial picture.

The auditor general reports that local level expenditures favor social development (44.29%), followed by infrastructure (27.05%), and management and administration (17.44%).[8] This emphasis differs somewhat from the economic focus at the provincial level, as might be expected based on the new functional

---

[8]   Government of Nepal, Auditor General Nepal. 2020. *Audit Report 2019/20.*

Table 2: Provincial Budgeted Expenditures, Fiscal Year 2021

Provinces	1	2	Bagmati	Gandaki	Karnali	Lumbini	Su.Paschim
Total Budget (NRs million)	40,900	33,400	51,427	34,499	33,311	36,352	33,081
Sector-Wise Budget Allotment (%)							
Economic Affairs (%)	32	33	45	50	37	33	26
General Public Service	26	52	41	26	34	46	53
Housing and Community Service	24	2	7	6	2	8	5
Health	6	5	2	4	6	4	7
Environment/Edu/Social Sec	6	5	2	2	1	2	2
Others	6	3	3	12	20	7	7
Total %	100	100	100	100	100	100	100

Source: Government of Nepal (provincial budget documents and sector budget allocations).

assignment. Useful comparisons are not possible as of 2021 given the dearth of data and level of aggregation.

Available data suggest that SNG spending in total is growing but is not offset by a reduction in federal government spending. As federalism implementation progressed to encompass provincial budgets (starting FY2019), the budget for SNGs increased significantly (Figure 2). In FY2019, the budget reached 12%

Figure 2: Budget Allocation to Provinces, Fiscal Years 2018–2021

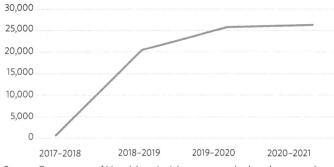

Source: Government of Nepal (provincial government budget documents).

of GDP, based on 36% of total government expenditures. This is in line with many counties with multilevel governments, but the lack of the corresponding reduction in national government spending as SNG budgets increased has fueled fiscal deficits[9] and caused the debt-to-GDP ratio to rise from about 25% in 2017 to 41% in 2020.[10]

The share of SNG expenditure in Nepal—40.5% of total public expenditure—corresponds to 16.2% of GDP. This could be considered low as Nepal is now a federal state; federal countries of the Organization for Economic Cooperation and Development boast of SNG expenditure of 50.1% of total public expenditure and 19.3% of GDP.[11] Considering the stage of economic development, however, the proportions suggest that Nepal considers the role of the state to be important. Should SNG expenditures continue to rise—to better reflect constitutional functional assignment—fiscal deficits and debt sustainability may become more problematic unless there is a corresponding reduction in federal expenditures.

9   International Monetary Fund (IMF). 2019. Nepal: Selected Issues. Journal Article A002. https://www.elibrary.imf.org/view/journals/002/2019/061/article-A002-en.xml.
10 Statista. Economy and Politics database (accessed October 2021).
11 Organization for Economic Cooperation and Development (OECD). 2021. OECD Regions and Cities at a Glance 2020; Subnational government spending (accessed October 2021).

Table 3: Staff Allocation and Vacancies in Provinces, 2019–2020

Provinces	Offices (Nos.)	Approved Positions	Share %	Filled Positions	Karnali	Filled %	Vacancies
No. 1	183	3,882	16	2,470	16	63.6	1,412
No. 2	129	3,034	13	2,094	14	69.0	940
Bagmati	191	3,875	16	2,582	17	66.6	1,293
Gandaki	153	2,813	12	2,039	13	72.5	774
Lumbini	182	4,414	19	2,568	17	58.2	1,846
Karnali Sudur	128	2,555	11	1,557	10	60.9	998
Paschim	129	3,115	13	2,133	14	68.5	982
Total	1095	23,688	100	15,443	100	65.2	8,245

Source: Annual Audit Report 2019/20, Office of the Auditor General, Nepal.

Nepal's expenditures per capita as a share of GDP compare well with neighboring countries, but its low level of GDP per capita overstates performance. Nepal's government expenditures have not shown a smooth upward trend as might be expected as a country develops. Even so, it attained expenditures equivalent to 21.1% of GDP in 2019, higher than regional comparators: Bangladesh (9.4%) and India (15.7%).[12] The GDP per capita, however, is lower at $1,195 than its regional neighbors (Bhutan, for instance, is nearly $3,000), meaning that expenditures per citizen are low. For instance, the government of Nepal is only able to pay for 25% of health care expenditures, leaving the rest to out-of-pocket coverage or other sources.[13]

SNGs have faced challenges in absorbing their allocations, principally due to capacity limitations and the disruptions of the COVID-19 pandemic. While SNGs made significant progress in establishing budget procedures, they have not been able to fully absorb their budgets. Actual expenditure as a percentage of the allocated budget for provincial governments improved from 43.59% in FY2018 to 54.50% in FY2019. However, it fell sharply to 20.19% in FY2020 because of the COVID-19 pandemic-related lockdowns in the months following March 2020. The low realization of the budget also reflects the late flow of funds to implementing agencies of SNGs; the bulk of expenditures is made in the last quarter.

Increasing budgets place more stress on SNGs to spend in this limited time frame. For newly established provinces—with large staff vacancies in their formation—it is difficult to ramp up spending capacity. Provinces face an average employee vacancy rate of about 35%, with Lumbini Province experiencing a high vacancy rate of 42% (Table 3). A similar situation is found at the local level, where the approved number of positions for the combined seven provinces

Table 4: Summary of Staff Allocation and Vacancies, 2019

Levels	Position Approved	Positions Adjusted/ Filled	Filled/ Adjusted %	Share % Level Wise
Federal	48,409	39,960	83	35
Province	22,297	13,821	62	16
Local	66,908	43,807	65	49
Aggregate	137,614	97,588	71	100

Source: Report of High-Level Administrative Reform Monitoring Committee 2019 (2076), pp. 212–213.

12   World Bank. Worldwide Indicators Database (accessed October 2021).
13   Government of Nepal, Nepal Renewable Energy Program. 2021. *A Note on Conditional Grant Renewable Energy Budget to Local Governments of Province 2*, Lumbini Province and Karnali Province. Kathmandu. https://www.nrepnepal.com/wp-content/uploads/2021/04/A-Note-on-Conditional-Grant-Renewable-Energy-Budget-to-Local-Governments-of-Province-2-Lumbini-Province-and-Karnali-Province.pdf.

was 66,908 (in 2019); out of this, only 43,807 (65%) were filled (Table 4). Keeping in mind the many changes set in motion at the SNG level by the federal transition (e.g., boundaries, organizations, functions, and a return of elected officials), SNGs face many challenges in forging effective organizations that can deliver on the high expectations that come with the federal restructuring.

There are no comprehensive studies available as of 2021 that seek to ascertain the constitutionally desired equalization effect of federal or provincial grants. As per the new Constitution, the distribution of the fiscal equalization grants should be based on expenditure needs and revenue sources. The challenges in sorting out expenditure needs have already been alluded to in terms of the complications of concurrence (para. 2). Additionally, there has been little effort placed on the cost of the constitutional mandates and assignment of expenditure functions and the improvements called for in meeting service standards or Sustainable Development Goal targets.

Revenue capacity is also challenging, and governments tend to focus on proxy measures such as regional GDP. It is not clear if Nepal has set up a data system that can ensure equalization through the grant system. Moreover, the federal government has relied more on conditional grants than equalization grants, contrary to the expectations of SNGs. Conditional grants themselves could be infused with equalization principles, but again it does not seem that this has been attempted. For example, the renewable energy grant to local governments does not appear to have electricity access as a grant indicator (footnote 13).

Examining expenditure data as presented in Table 5, there is considerable variation in per capita expenditures by province, with Karnali spending four times more than Province 2. Karnali also receives twice the revenue (except for grants) than Province 2. This information shows that there is a disparity in spending and own revenues but does not speak to the equalization effect of grants; whether they work to close these gaps or aggravate disparities. Initial studies on equalization suggest that the allocation formula and methodology used for the distribution of the fiscal equalization grants need to be reviewed as it has been perceived to be unequal, not objective, and unfair. For example, Province 2 received the lowest grant of all provinces, but it is the second largest province in terms of population and

Table 5: Per Capita Provincial Expenditures and Revenues 2019–2020 (NRs'000)

Provinces	Population ('000) (2011)	Share %	Expenditure	Share %	Per Capita Expenditure	Revenue Received (Except Grants)	Per Capita Revenue
No. 1	4,534	17.1	29,833,200	19.1	6,580	10,706,700	2,361
No. 2	5,404	20.4	18,017,200	11.5	3,334	9,809,800	1,815
Bagmati	5,529	20.9	27,950,800	17.9	5,055	21,536,700	3,895
Gandaki	2,414	9.1	20,413,600	13.1	8,456	7,374,000	3,055
Lumbini	4,891	18.5	25,407,100	16.3	5,195	10,193,200	2,084
Karnali							
Sudur Pashchim	2,553	9.6	17,611,900	11.3	6,899	6,877,100	
Total	26,494	100.0	156,114,000	100.0	5,892	71,719,200	2,707

Source: Government of Nepal, Financial Comptroller General Office/Ministry of Finance. 2020. Office of the Auditor General, Nepal Financial Statement FY2020 and Audit Report.

the worst ranked in poverty and other human development-related indicators.[14]

The Government of Nepal has sought to improve the efficiency of SNG spending. Several initiatives have contributed to this effort, including the following:

(i) **Guiding SNGs on their organizational structures.** SNGs have established organizations based on the structures approved by the Cabinet, beginning with those issued for provinces in June 2017. MOFAGA issued these, encompassing structures and staffing levels based on the expected workload and the size of the population. It is not clear whether the workload was derived based on the new functional load. SNGs have the legal right to adjust these organizations but it is not clear that they are taking advantage of this option, which can be pursued based on an organization and management survey (LGO Act, 2017, Section 83).

(ii) **Providing annual budget and MTEF guidelines and templates oriented to the SNG context.** To attain uniformity and effective budgets, the MOFAGA issued the Local Level Budget Formulation Guideline 2018 to local governments, consistent with the budget calendar for all three levels of government (Appendixes 3-5). Many local governments have issued their budget and program formulation guidelines to concerned departments, wards, agencies, and communities. All seven provinces prepared an initial MTEF with a 3-year rolling timeline. However, these lacked a multiyear perspective and linkages to an annual budget.[15] The adoption of MTEF at the local government level was in its infancy as of 2021 as the capacities of local governments were still being developed.[16]

(iii) **Creating an e-Government Procurement (e-GP) system** for use by all public entities across the country including at the subnational level for procurement activities.[17] Directives issued by the Public Procurement Management Office in 2017 made it mandatory to use the e-GP system for procurements above a certain threshold amount.[18]

(iv) **Supporting the use of the SuTRA.** SuTRA is a planning, budgeting, accounting, and reporting software. It covers transactions related to the local treasury system including budget, expenditure, and revenue. The development of this system is expected to provide the government with the means of fine-tuning its equalization grants.

(v) **Developing a comprehensive ICT-based online Nepal audit management system covering the whole audit life cycle of the Office of the Auditor General of Nepal.** The system has been developed and is ready

---

[14] K.L. Devkota. 2020. Intergovernmental Fiscal Transfers in a Federal Nepal. *International Center for Public Policy Working Paper Series*, Working Paper 20-17. Atlanta: International Center for Public Policy, Andrew Young School of Policy Studies, Georgia State University.

[15] ADB. 2017. *Policy and Advisory Technical Assistance 9150 Nepal: Strengthening Subnational Public Management Revised Draft Midterm Report.* Manila.

[16] Government of Nepal, Office of the Auditor General. 2020. *57th Annual Audit Report of the Auditor General, 2077*; Discussion with officials of the Ministry of Federal Affairs and General Administration.

[17] Established by the Public Procurement Monitoring Office with assistance from ADB through the Strengthening Public Management Program.

[18] The threshold amounts are (i) above NRs20 million ($200,000) for works; (ii) above NRs6 million ($60,000) for goods; and (iii) above NRs2 million ($20,000) for consulting services.

for piloting as of 2021. Once rolled out, cost centers associated with all levels of government that are under the audit purview of the Office of the Auditor General will be audited using this system.

Key Challenges in Public Expenditure and Budgeting

The scope of the reforms bound to the shift to the new federal constitutional order has been broad and deep, and this has at times overstretched the capacity of the federal government and SNGs. The lack of an overall implementation plan that would have prioritized and sequenced key reforms has led to many reforms being managed at once but with few finding the depth of implementation desired. For example, SNGs were expected to adjust their organizational structures and staffing to conform to schedules of functions that were not yet

BOX 3
Introducing Medium-Term Expenditure Frameworks— International Experience

By 2003, municipalities were also mandated to apply it; however, at this level, the effectiveness of the MTEF was undermined by the lack of predictability in transfers. Other countries have struggled to introduce this tool in a meaningful way where progress has been made at the national level. With the benefit of this experience, proponents suggest capacity and system requisites for introducing the MTEF and conclude that countries should be cautious about moving too quickly unless and until their basic systems of budgeting are working well.

As Nepal was in flux on budget processes, and capacities were strained and rather weak to begin with—particularly at the SNG level—the introduction of the MTEF was premature

Source: R. Allen et al. 2017. Medium-Term Budget Frameworks in Selected Sub-Saharan African Countries. *IMF Working Paper* 17/203. Washington, DC: IMF.

clarified while strengthening internal governance processes. These processes included efforts such as applying MTEF approaches to planning and budgeting, and the SuTRA planning, budgeting, and reporting software.

Such systems can be well designed but require some capacity and basic systems—and stability in institutions—to take hold (Box 3). The capacity challenges were further exacerbated by the unforeseen impact of the COVID-19 pandemic starting in early 2020. It is not surprising that the MTEF, SuTRA, and other initiatives continue to be works in progress that are progressing only as quickly as capacities can be developed in the new institutions. Local governments have limited capacity to estimate future revenues and expenditure and monitor performance by departments and outcomes achieved.

The effort to establish new institutional arrangements and practices calls for good coordination horizontally at the federal level and with supporting partners. The focus—stemming from the Constitution—has been to establish robust intergovernmental mechanisms, but this can only work well when the key coordinating ministries and agencies offer coherent guidance. In designing new governance elements for SNGs in the context of federalism, the federal government could have paid more attention to coordinating the national agencies. For instance, the differences between the MOFAGA and the MOF over the choice of financial management software—referred to as the Municipal Administration and Revenue System (MARS) versus the SuTRA—led to unnecessary waste of effort, money, and time.[19]

The kind of horizontal coordination needed can be facilitated by development partners. Conversely, initiatives that seek to promote

---

[19] The ministry responsible for SNGs at the time (the Ministry of Federal Affairs and Local Development) had intended to test and disseminate the ADB-supported MARS, whereas the Ministry of Finance sought to promote and disseminate the SuTRA application.

specific solutions advanced by development partners working in isolation can hinder the kind of coordination needed to design and disseminate new systems coherently. In the case of MARS versus SuTRA, development partners were split in their support, making it harder for Government of Nepal organizations to converge on a choice.[20]

Uncertainty over who has the responsibility for expenditure functions between the provincial and local levels is hampering the efficient delivery of public services. The federal government is still taking the lead—or playing an inordinate role—in many sectors and services that are legally ostensibly in the hands of SNGs. A reading of the national budget documents attests to the micromanagement that takes place in contradiction with the intergovernmental assignment of functions.[21] The ad hoc approach to addressing the threat of COVID-19 suggests that systems to apportion roles and coordinate in the health system are still in the early stages. The COVID-19 response revealed that "Each government level and hospital seems to be confused about the discharge of its respective roles."[22] Local governments were belatedly pushed to form tracing committees to play a role in the effort. Moreover, local governments do not appear to be doing enough to monitor the claims of alternative health practitioners or act against the spread of misinformation about treatments for COVID-19.[23]

The lack of clarity over which functions "must" be performed (versus "may" be performed) and the performance expectations for these mandated functions weakens accountability. There is little work being done to clarify the performance standards that apply to services that have been devolved to SNGs. This hesitancy relates in part to concurrence challenges. For instance, community infrastructure, urban and settlement development, housing, and infrastructure development are concurrent responsibilities. Their definition, standards, and classification have not been clarified.[24] Making them clear would require sorting out specific roles and interconnections or coordination mechanisms between the three levels of government. In turn, a decision would need to be made on whether the roles are prescribed, and what support and sanctions would apply for noncompliance. If there are consequences for nonperformance, standards would need to be set carefully to reflect the technical and financial capacities of SNGs. This would reduce unrealistic standards or the dropping of expectations simply to clear the lowest performers (which would not meet the intent of the rights-based constitutional provisions on service provision).

The broad reforms on expenditure management related to the shift in federalism have not yet answered some of the perennial public financial management challenges in Nepal. For instance, a disproportionate amount of expenditure occurs in the last trimester of the financial year, which leads to the ineffective utilization of resources due to hasty implementation. The COVID-19 lockdowns in FY2020 exacerbated this disbursement and budget utilization problem. Inadequate

20   Independent Evaluation Department. 2019. *Validation Report—Nepal: Strengthening Public Management Program.* Appendix 1. Manila: ADB.
21   See, e.g., the National Budget 2021–2022, which contains such items as the midday meal program for students. https://nepaleconomicforum.org/neftake/nepal-budget-for-fiscal-year-2021-22/.
22   Government of Nepal, National Disaster Risk Reduction Centre. 2020. *Nepal's Readiness and Response to COVID-19: Key Initiatives, Emergency Challenges, and the Way Forward.* Kathmandu.
23   B. Rayamajhee et al. 2021. How Well the Government of Nepal Is Responding to COVID-19? An Experience from a Resource-Limited Country to Confront Unprecedented Pandemic. *Front Public Health.* 17 February.
24   AusAid and The Asia Foundation. 2019. *Functional Assignment Across Spheres of Government.* Paper prepared for a Policy Dialogue. Kathmandu. 30 July.

alignment of policies, plans, budgets, and insufficient vertical coordination persist from previous times. This also applies to weaknesses in project preparedness, procurement, contract management, and the oversight of expenditures.

The challenge of inadequate human resources in the SNGs was felt before the reforms related to federalism. The state restructuring entailed by federalism has largely shifted the human resources gaps; these are now most keenly felt at the provincial and local levels. The constitutional requirement to achieve good governance—particularly in addressing corrupt practices—has yet to receive an adequate answer in the new institutions and practices following federalism. Local and provincial internal audit systems to improve transparency in public financial management at the subnational level need strengthening.

The broader institutional framework and capacity for accountability for SNG spending are still being developed. After 15 years without SNG elections, it will take some time for a new culture of local electoral accountability to take hold. Successful accountability will require suitable top–down mechanisms operating between levels of government and bottom–up mechanisms that orient SNGs to citizens. The new legal framework has ensured some vertical top–down mechanisms such as auditing by the auditor general and public recourse to the Commission for the Investigation of Abuse of Authority. But some parts of the legal framework are undeveloped or interpreted in different ways. For instance, the constitutional interpretation that local government is prevented from providing payment for political representatives may be counterproductive, encouraging corruption rather than limiting it.[25] Mechanisms for coordination between levels of government during budget preparation also remain underdeveloped.[26]

Bottom–up mechanisms had been developed in the past, particularly social accountability practices (public hearing or public audit, budget tracking, and citizen scorecard).[27] The role of these mechanisms in the new federal system is unclear, as are participatory planning, transparency of financial information, gender-based budgeting, and other governance processes that potentially make SNGs responsive and responsible for performance. These mechanisms work best when there is also horizontal accountability between the local councils (legislature) and the executive branch of SNGs. In areas of public financial management where systems and procedures are in place, capacities to realize them in practice often vary widely. For instance, the Office of the Auditor General in its Annual Report 2019 notes that only 298 out of 753 SNGs submitted a consolidated report of funds and treasury positions using SuTRA, with reporting formats often diverging from those prescribed by the Office of the Auditor General.[28]

Addressing these weaknesses will require building local capacities, but also changing the way systems are developed to ensure that they have the flexibility and relevance needed to be absorbed by SNGs.

[25]   See, for instance, the Supreme Court's ruling against provincial efforts to rectify this shortcoming in R.K. Kamat. 2019. *SC Halts Salaries of Local Level Office Bearers.* The Himalayan, 19 October.

[26]   Government of Nepal, National Planning Commission. 2021. *48th NDAC Report. National Development Action Committee* (in original language).

[27]   See, for instance, K. Khadka and C. Bhattarai. 2012. *Source Book of 21 Social Accountability Tools.* Kathmandu: Program for Accountability in Nepal.

[28]   N. Jha. 2020. Reforming Local Governments' Accountability Practices. Econity. 15 August. https://econitynepal.com/reforming-local-governments-accountability-practices/.

Recommendations to Improve Expenditure Assignment and Budgeting

Much remains to be done to elaborate governance systems in line with constitutional requirements and good practice. These efforts should aim to achieve greater discretion for SNGs while increasing their accountability. The following steps—requiring federal government initiative or leadership—are urgent.

(i) Clarify the assignment of functions for provincial and local governments, and linking these to financing sources—i.e., revenue assignments and transfers—that are in line with the weight and nature of the functions assigned to SNGs.

(ii) Set performance expectations of SNG expenditure functions and the mechanisms through which SNGs will be incentivized or sanctioned.

(iii) Orient budgeting to be more output- and outcome-oriented, particularly for those functions that have stringent performance expectations.

(iv) Enhance intergovernmental coordination to ensure that federal and SNGs are focusing on their respective functions and that there is avoidance of duplication (unless concurrence is intended, and interlocking and coordinated).

(v) Review and amend laws and regulations that are still current but are contradictory to the emerging assignment of functions (e.g., infusing these laws and regulations with the consensus of lists generated in the unbundling exercise).

(vi) Inform the public about the new responsibilities of the government and facilitating the application of the social accountability movement in Nepal for making SNGs accountable for their new functions.

(vii) Enhance the internal audit system in provinces and local governments where these are inadequate.

Given the extensive reforms and capacity development that remain unfinished in expenditure assignment and planning and budgeting, it will be important to set priorities commensurate with the emerging capacities of the federal government and SNGs. This will mean setting priorities and sequencing reforms based on ongoing assessments of capacity. For example, this approach may reveal that a phased adoption of MTEFs at the SNG level is appropriate. The provincial and local governments should be supported to establish a functioning annual budgeting process that is linked to periodic and annual planning. With that in place, a phased approach to adopting the MTEF approach by SNGs should be attempted, with strong support from national agencies that will have had considerable experience in applying it nationally by that time.

The Government of Nepal should develop a more robust and long-term approach to capacity development relating to public expenditure and budgeting. An important step has been made in this regard, with the strengthening of provincial training bodies. These need to be further strengthened to serve provincial and local governments. The restructured federal Local Development Training Academy should refocus on the capacity development of federal representatives and bureaucrats as well as provide technical assistance to provincial training centers.

CHAPTER IV

REVENUE MOBILIZATION

Revenue mobilization of SNGs is essential for the success of fiscal federalism in Nepal. Revenue that is commensurate with the assigned functions will facilitate the fulfillment of constitutional guarantees and the specific responsibilities of each level of government. A meaningful level of own source revenue (OSR) will enable SNGs to be responsive to local needs and exercise a high level of discretion—with accountability—in delivering services and undertaking other development activities.

Legally Mandated Revenue Functions of SNGs

The Constitution of Nepal calls for the equitable distribution of revenues between the federal, provincial, and local governments. A general assignment is found within the constitutional schedules listing the powers and jurisdictions (functions) (Table 6). Revenue assignment is elaborated on in legislation.

The considerable degree of concurrence in the assignment of revenue functions is partly managed through legislation that addresses the revenue split between provincial and local governments. Lists of revenue rights for the three levels of government exhibit considerable overlaps, which can potentially become points of tension. Appendix 6 shows where ostensibly "exclusive" rights of provincial and local governments overlap, and where the rights of all three levels of government appear to overlap. Local government and finance acts provide additional details on which level of government sets the rates, collects the revenue, and how the revenue is shared. This further elaboration largely resolves the considerable overlap in the taxation rights assigned to provincial and local governments (Table 7).

Table 6: Revenue Rights Listed Commonly in More than One Schedule

Center (Schedule 5)	Provinces (Schedule 6)	Local Level (Schedule 8)
Custom duty	Vehicle tax	Vehicle tax
VAT	Entertainment tax	Entertainment tax
Excise duty	Advertisement tax	Advertisement tax
Corporate income tax	House and land registration fee	House and land registration fee
Individual income tax	Agricultural income tax	Property tax
Remuneration tax		House rent tax
		Business tax
		Land tax (land revenue)

Source: ADB. 2018. Consultant's Report (PATA 9150) Strengthening Subnational Public Management in Nepal. Manila.

Table 7: Revenue Administration Arrangement across Levels of Government

Sl. No.	Taxes	Set Rates	Collect	Regulate & Administer	Distribution		Remarks
					P	L	
1	House and land registration fee[a]	P	L	F, P, L	40	60	Malpot (Land Revenue office collects at the time of registration)
2	Vehicle taxes a. Motor vehicle[a]	P	P	P	60	40	Presently, collected by Transportation Management Office
	b. Other vehicle[b]	L	L	L	–	100	
	c. Driving license and Bluebook renewal service fee	P	P	P	100	–	Presently, collected by Transportation Management Office
3	Entertainment tax[a]	P	L	L	40	60	
4	Advertisement tax[a]	P	L	L	40	60	
5	a. Tourism fee	P	P	P	100	–	Provincial tourism fee, collected by the provincial ministry
	b. Local tourism	L	L	L	40	60	
6	Fee on collection and sale of natural resources[c]	P	L	L	40	60	
7	Service charge and fee	F, P, L	F, P, L	F, P, L	–	–	Each level of government may impose service charges based on their laws. They define the base and rates. No distribution
8	Penalty	F, P, L	F, P, L	F, P, L	–	–	Each level of government may impose and collect penalties based on their laws. No distribution

F = Federal, P = Provincial, L = Local.

[a] At the time of collection, the amount is deposited into a provincial divisible fund, and after distribution of the tax it goes to the relevant consolidated fund.

[b] *Tanga*, rickshaw, auto-rickshaw, e-rickshaw, power teller.

[c] This includes only those natural resources for which fees are charged at the subnational level: sand, concrete, stones, boulders, crushed stones, and dahattar bahattar (river-based resources). The local government should submit an action plan of the environmental impact study for these to the provincial government.

Source: Constitution of Nepal, Intergovernmental Fiscal Management Act, 2017; Local Government Operation Act, 2017; Finance Act, 2019; and Finance Act, 2020; arranged by the team in tabular form.

Federal government taxes are more buoyant than those assigned to SNGs, causing a vertical fiscal imbalance. Taxation powers for customs duty, value-added tax (VAT), excise duty, corporate income tax, and individual income tax lie with the federal government. These taxes account for almost 80% of total tax revenue. They are—in general—more buoyant than those assigned to SNGs (e.g., vehicle, land, property, and entertainment). In FY2017, the VAT—the largest tax source—grew by 31.3% as imports climbed, continuing the trend. Customs duties showed strong growth at 36.7% and income taxes at 26.6%. A proportion of federal government-assigned revenues are shared with SNGs, but the bulk remains at the federal level.

Some SNG taxes are reasonably buoyant, but others present challenges in their collection. Entertainment and advertisement taxes can be buoyant. However, with the decrease in tourism brought about by the COVID-19 pandemic, these taxes may be suppressed, at least for FY2021. Other SNG taxes—like the agriculture income tax (exclusive to the provincial government)—also face challenges. In the case of the agriculture income tax, individuals have been exempted from it when the tax was the responsibility of the central government.

As of 2021, provinces are devising different approaches to this tax, including not applying the tax, extending the tax to individuals, or commercial farmers only (Gandaki Province). In the case of Sudur Pashchim Province (Province 7) the tax was introduced in FY2020 but repealed the following year. Provinces are meeting with varying levels of success in tapping into this new source of revenue.

Non-tax revenues pertain to services falling under the jurisdictions of each level of government and are in principle tied to defraying the cost of services. Except for passport and visa fees, other non-tax sources are listed in the schedules of the Constitution that pertain to all three levels of government (Table 8). The sources are not specified; initially giving this construction the appearance of concurrence. However, understanding emerges in the Intergovernmental Fiscal Arrangement (IGFA) Act, 2017, where Schedules 2 and 3 specify that the province and local government are to relate their laws on non-tax revenues to matters falling under the province and local government's domain. In other words, service charges, fees, and penalties for services are provided by the respective governments. Moreover, service fees are to be levied based on the cost of providing services (IGFA Act, 2017, Section 4).

Royalties from natural resources and tourism fees relate to the same revenue base. They give rise to true concurrence and are listed in the concurrent list in Schedule 9 of the Constitution (Table 8). Consequently, ways of sharing these among the tiers of the government have been determined. Royalties collected from natural resources (including mountaineering) by the federal government are divided among governments in ratios of 50% (federal), 25% (provincial), and 25% (local) (IGFA Act, 2017, Section 7, Appendix 4). In the case of tourism, the provinces impose and collect tourism fees on tourism-related infrastructure transferred by the federal government to the provinces and

Table 8: Distribution of Non-Tax Revenue Sources as per the Constitution

Centre (Schedule 5)	Provinces (Schedule 6)	Local Level (Schedule 8)
Service charge and fee	Service charge and fee	Service charge and fee
Penalty	Penalty	Penalty
Tourism fee	Tourism fee	Tourism fee
Passport fee		
Visa fee		
Concurrent List (Schedule 9)		
Service fee, charge, penalties, royalty from natural resources, tourism fee		

Source: ADB. 2018. *PATA 9150 Strengthening Subnational Public Management in Nepal.*

infrastructure developed by the provinces. The municipality (rural and urban) may levy and collect fees on aggregates, cable cars, trekking, kayaking, canoeing, bungee jumping, zip flyers, rafting, paragliding, and other local tourism, entertainment, and adventure sports-related service or business operating in its area (LGO Act, 2017, Section 62).

Findings on Revenue Mobilization at the Subnational Level

Government revenue collection improved during 2010–2020 but is still insufficient to ensure that expenditure functions assigned to SNGs are well funded. The government of Nepal has managed to raise revenues to the equivalent of about 22% of GDP, which compares well with a South Asia average of 12% in 2019. Nepal is heavily reliant on borrowing and foreign grants, with revenues estimated for FY2021 to account for only 61% of total resources (Figure 3).[29] This would be significantly lower than the actual achieved in FY2020 of 86%.[30] The COVID-19 pandemic slowed growth in 2020–2021, affecting revenue collection from sectors like tourism. The government will find it difficult to adequately fund SNGs commensurate with the expenditure functions that have been assigned to them.

A persistent vertical fiscal imbalance places urgency on raising SNG revenues, but this has proven difficult to do. Under its federal design, Nepal's vertical fiscal gap is one of the largest among federal countries with upwards of 85% of revenues flowing to the federal government.[31] As the functional assignment is suggestive of a pyramid structure—with the local government bearing the bulk of service delivery—this

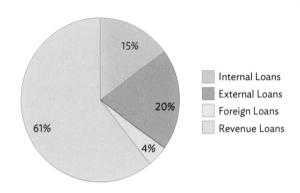

Figure 3: Percentage Share of Government Resources, Fiscal Year 2021 (Based on the Budget Estimation)

Source: Bista and Ghimire. 2020. National Budget 2020/21: An Analytical Review. Nepal Economic Forum. 29 May.

construction leaves SNGs dependent on federal transfers. SNGs collect 15% of overall government revenues but account for 36% of spending. This expenditure share likely underestimates the vertical fiscal imbalance as there has not been an attempt to cost the functions assigned to SNGs.

The majority of SNG finances come from federal government transfers. The imbalance would be more severe if SNG functions were to be costed to meet service delivery expectations, and the additional funds were to come from the federal government rather than local revenues. SNGs have been making efforts to boost their revenues to close this gap (Box 4) with some success. This has come largely at a local level.

Table 9 provides the provincial and local revenues for FY2019 and FY2020. The provincial level shows a decrease, and the local level a significant increase. The combined level of 5.47% of GDP for SNGs is a small share of the 22% of GDP achieved by the government,

---

[29] I. Bista and S. Ghimire. 2020. National Budget 2020/21: An Analytical Review. *Nepal Economic Forum*. 29 May.
[30] Government of Nepal, Financial Comptroller General Office/Ministry of Finance. 2020. Financial Statement/ Income and Expenditure FY2020. Part 1, p. 11.
[31] World Bank. 2017. *Nepal Development Update*.

BOX 4
Nepal Subnational Government Efforts to Increase Revenue

Tax officials have requested local chambers of commerce in the municipalities of Banepa (Butwal sub-metropolitan city) and Dhulikhel (Lalitpur metropolitan city) for records of businesses run in their jurisdiction so that they can more accurately determine tax liability. Moreover, they have reached out to taxpayers through radio broadcasts, emphasizing deadlines for tax payment and rebates for early payment of taxes.

Other municipalities are also moving toward greater digitization for tax collection. Computerized receipts for tax payments are being issued to wards (a division of local government), enabling the local government to obtain real-time information on revenue collection at the ward level.

Source: ADB. 2016. *TA:9150—NEP: Strengthening Subnational Public Management in Nepal.* Manila.

Table 9: Provincial and Local Revenues as a Percentage of Gross Domestic Product, Fiscal Years 2019 and 2020

Province	FY2019	FY2020
Province 1	0.31	0.28
Province 2	0.26	0.26
Bagmati Province	0.52	0.57
Gandaki Province	0.25	0.19
Lumbini Province	0.29	0.26
Karnali Province	0.15	0.14
Sudurpashchim Province	0.2	0.17
Total of 7 provinces	1.98	1.87
Total of 752 local levels	2.17	3.6
SNGS Total	4.16	5.47

Source: Government of Nepal, Financial Comptroller General Office/Ministry of Finance. 2020. Financial Statement (Income and Expenditure), FY2019 and FY2020.

essentially continuing with the fiscal gap that was evident before federalism. While it is fair to expect SNGs to make the most of their existing or new revenue-raising powers, revenue mobilization could continue to lag if SNGs are dependent on transfers to close the fiscal gap.[32] Ways of incentivizing revenue efforts need to be found, or ways to enlarge the sources available to SNGs.

Horizontal imbalances in revenue mobilization—present before federalism—continue to be evident. There is considerable inequity in revenue generation between provinces (Table 5). It is not clear what is driving the differences in revenues (per capita) across the SNGs. It is likely to be a story about economic endowments as well as capacity and political willingness (tax effort). Typically, SNGs vary in the efficiency of revenue efforts based on cumbersome systems of tax collection, slow reaction to tax arrears, corrupt practices, low technical skills among tax officials, and limited use of modern information technology systems. Some of these capacity differences can be overcome with local effort and support from higher levels of government. Ultimately, equalizing grants will be needed to reduce the remaining gaps.

The most important source of revenue for local government remains fiscal transfers and revenue sharing. Given the relatively small share of own revenues, fiscal transfers and revenue sharing are left to play the major role in enabling local government to deliver services equitably across Nepal. Own source revenue (OSR) remains below 10% for local government (Table 10). Grants play a major role at this level (78%) and revenue sharing is much less but still significant (14%). Grants are considerably lower

---

[32] Literature has generally pointed to the crowding out effect of transfers on local revenue raising, but there is some emerging evidence that the effect can be positive, i.e., a crowding in effect. See T. Masaki. 2018. The Impact of Intergovernmental Transfers on Local Revenue Generation in Sub-Saharan Africa: Evidence from Tanzania. *Science Direct.* Vol. 106(C). pp. 173–186.

in provinces (about 40%). Revenue sharing is about the same, and OSR is about 20% (Appendix 7).

Intergovernmental friction around the demarcation of rights to raise revenue has arisen, particularly concerning concurrent revenue rights. The LGO Act, 2017 adds detail on expenditure and revenue assignments for local governments. It allows local governments to raise revenue from the sale of natural resources, including soil, sand, rocks, and other items. However, a few provinces have introduced legislation—presumably based on their responsibility for royalties or fees on natural resources—allowing the district coordination committees to raise such taxes, although the committees are only coordinating bodies of the province and are not revenue-raising institutions.[33] In another sector, some municipalities have started to charge tourism fees to visitors entering their jurisdictions, citing the Schedule 7 list in the Constitution as their legal support. In November 2017, the Ministry of Federal Affairs and Local Development issued a notice, directing all the local levels not to collect a "tourism fee" from any visitor. But some local governments hold that the constitutional list trumps any such federal order.[34]

Reform Initiatives and Challenges in Improving Revenue Mobilization

Nepal took large strides during 2010–2020 to improve its revenue administration, and this effort has continued in the transition to federalism. Supported by many development partners, Nepal has made legislative changes to fine-tune certain taxes (Appendix 8) and

Table 10: Local Government Own Revenues Relative to All Sources of Revenue, Fiscal Years 2019 and 2020

Revenue Heads	FY201 (NRs billion)	Approved Positions	Share %	Filled Positions
Revenue sharing[a]	48.79	54.15	14	15
Own source revenue	26.73	30.53	8	9
Grants[b]	265.94	265.95	78	76
Total	341.46	350.63	100	100

Note: Numbers may not sum precisely because of rounding.
[a] Includes sharing from provinces.
[b] Includes federal and provincial grants.
Source: Government of Nepal, Office of the Auditor General.

boosted its revenues by 12.8 percentage points against GDP during 2007–2019, reaching about 22%.[35] Continued growth at this pace will be challenging because of the enhanced role of SNGs in the reassigned revenue functions. SNGs will also need to join in the effort to regulate and administer revenue, including setting tax rates (where given latitude), conducting studies of revenue potential, and building institutional and human capacity to match their ambitions.

The government is seeking to improve provincial and local government revenue administration but faces considerable challenges. These challenges relate to the institutional framework required to boost revenues, and the operational and management challenges to make the most of these frameworks. Among these are the following:

(i)   Lack of adequate capacity at provincial and local levels to assess the revenue potential, determine the effective tax rate, and forecast future revenues and tax gaps of their local governments.

(ii)   A slowdown in some taxes and fees where these are linked to sectors

[33]   M. Acharya et al. 2020. *Assignment of Functions Across Levels of Government in Nepal.* Kathmandu: Creative Press Pvt. Ltd.
[34]   Kathmandu Post. 2017. Local Govts Defy Centre's Order on "Tourism Fee." 8 November.
[35]   B. Akitoby et al. 2020. Tax Revenues in Fragile and Conflict-Affected States —Why Are They Low and How Can We Raise Them? *IMF Working Paper* 20/143. Washington, DC: IMF.

heavily impacted by the COVID-19 pandemic (e.g., tourism).

(iii) Low levels of tax administration capacity of local government; many assigned taxes saw a dip in collection following restructuring.[36]

(iv) Unclear demarcation—in some instances—of the revenue rights of the levels of government for non-tax revenue sources like service fees or penalties.

(v) A tendency for provincial governments to increase rates rather than enlarge the tax base and coverage.

(vi) Overreliance on natural resource taxes—such as sand, gravel, and stone tax—and the royalties from natural resources—such as forests and rivers—as potential sources of revenue may have severe environmental repercussions in the long run.

(vii) Local fees are levied without adequate consideration of taxpayer ability to pay. A striking example is the charge of NRs1,000 for birth registration.

(viii) Lack of adequate systems to address the grievances of taxpayers. There is also no provision for taxpayers to pay taxes in installments.

The federal government has taken steps to address some of the above challenges, many of which are aligned with international best practices. These include the following:

(i) Formulation of "Model Acts and Rules" to ensure provinces can adopt robust laws and rules and avoid unhealthy competition (Appendix 9).

(ii) Setting up a suitable institutional mechanism for compilation and collation of fiscal data including subnational revenue data. The provincial line ministry budget information system is used for provincial level programming, planning, and budgeting. At the local level, the SuTRA has been implemented with the assistance of the Financial Comptroller General Office (FCGO). This application is used by local governments in planning, budgeting, accounting, and reporting. More than 740 local governments have entered records of financial transactions in this application for FY2020 and reported their financial information to concerned agencies accordingly, while all 753 local governments used SuTRA to formulate the budget for FY2021.[37] The use of SuTRA is mandatory for local governments.

(iii) Development of mechanisms for tax assessment and facilitation of registration, filing of returns, and the provision of information by the SNGs. The mechanisms have been incorporated into the legal and policy framework through the Tax and Non-Tax Revenue Act. However, there is scope for further enhancement of the capacities of the SNGs and digitization of the mechanism.

(iv) Incorporating "revenue effort" as a criterion in revenue sharing formulas between the three levels of government. As per Section 15 of the NNRFC Act, 2017, NNRFC determines the bases and measures of the distribution of revenue among the federal, provincial, and local governments and the measures are to be determined based on the indicators related to population and demographic factors, area, human development index, expenditure need, revenue collection effort, and development of infrastructures and specific conditions. On 13 March 2020, NNRFC

---

[36] According to an estimate by the NNRFC, total revenue loss in FY2019—after the transfer of tax jurisdictions from federal to SNGs—was NRs51 billion. See B. Bhurtel. 2019. *Fiscal Federalism: An Analysis of Its Initial Implementation in Nepal.* London: International Alert.

[37] Government of Nepal: 2020. Consolidated Financial Statement, 2019–2020.

recommended a 3% weightage for "revenue effort" in the revenue sharing formula for FY2021.[38]

(v) Training of revenue officials on revenue mobilization of SNGs. Provincial and local governments have conducted short-term training based on their responsibilities and tasks.

Recommendations

The Constitution gives the federal government—and to some extent the provincial government—a role in shaping the revenue framework of the local government, where most services will in principle be delivered. The reforms and improvements will need to further clarify the rights and discretion of federal, provincial, and local governments in revenue functions and administration. Moreover, the framework developed will need to strengthen the local government's accountability to the citizens who must contribute to its revenues and are the beneficiaries of revenue deriving from higher levels of government.

Emphasis is warranted on the following efforts, to be led by the federal government:

(i) Review and amendment of laws and policies to ensure clarity and consistency in the demarcation of revenue rights of SNGs.

(ii) Assistance to SNGs to improve OSR by encouraging

(a) the linking of revenues to expenditures to promote efficiency, transparency, and accountability;

(b) pro-business policies at the local level to grow the sources of revenue;

(c) digitization of transactions and taxation systems; and

(d) the mounting of taxpayer awareness campaigns to strengthen the "fiscal contract" and establishing grievance redressal mechanisms to ensure fairness and willingness to pay.

(iii) Development of new sources of revenue for SNGs, possibly attached to federal taxes—like VAT, excise, income, and corporate income taxes—or by developing new taxes and non-tax sources such as carbon and pollution tax, congestion tax, water contamination tax, and annual fees from energy projects. Congestion taxes are particularly relevant in rapidly growing urban agglomerations with space constraints such as the Kathmandu Valley. The search for new sources of revenue should take second place in the effort to maximize the revenue sources already assigned.

---

[38] Revenue Effort is the ratio of actual revenue collected to the empirically estimated revenue capacity.

CHAPTER V

INTERGOVERNMENTAL FISCAL TRANSFERS

Legal and Institutional Arrangement of Fiscal Transfers

The Constitution of Nepal provides for intergovernmental fiscal transfers (IGFT) to reduce the gap between the expenditure needs arising from the functional responsibilities and revenue-raising rights given to SNGs. A well-formulated fiscal transfer mechanism is essential for reducing vertical and horizontal fiscal imbalances at the subnational levels of government. In this regard, the NNRFC Act, 2017, the Intergovernmental Fiscal Arrangement Act, 2017, and the LGO Act, 2017 provide the legal framework for fiscal transfers, defining the transfers and the distribution criteria for the two broad types of fiscal transfer: grants and revenue sharing. Provincial and local governments receive four types of grants: fiscal equalization, conditional, special, and matching grants.

In addition to equalization grants, other grants provided by the federal government are used to spur development or address specific provincial or local circumstances. These additional grants are conditional, matching, and special grants

(Table 11). NNRFC is tasked to conduct studies to prepare parameters for conditional grants based on national policies and programs, norms and standards, and infrastructure endowment.[39] Specific procedures are generally left to the MOF. Where grants are project-specific (matching and special grants), a project selection committee is formed under the chairship of a member of the NPC. Other members are a joint secretary from the MOF, a joint secretary from the Ministry of Federal Affairs and General Administration (MOFAGA), and a joint secretary from a concerned ministry.

The joint secretary responsible for the Infrastructure Division of the NPC plays the role of member secretary. The committee evaluates and selects the projects submitted by provincial and local governments in a portal specifically created (www.msgrants.gov.np).[40] Criteria and considerations provide the federal government with much discretion in setting these grants and the flexibility to change focus on an annual basis (Table 13). The flip side to this discretion and flexibility is the management capacity it requires of the federal government and the lack of predictability and room for inconsistent application in federal decision-making from

---

[39] Government of Nepal. Constitution of Nepal, Article 251(c).
[40] The portal for the submission of projects by provincial and local governments and the Project Selection Committee for Special Grants is similar to that for matching/complementary grants, the only difference being the member secretary—who in this case is the Joint Secretary—who looks after the Social Development Division of the National Planning Commission.

Table 11: Other Grants from Federal to Subnational Governments

Sr. No.	Source	Target Government	Criteria
1	Conditional grants	Provincial and local	(i) Welfare indicators (ii) Comparative level of development (iii) Discrimination experienced (iv) Infrastructure development and need (v) Services delivery burden (vi) Tax raising capacity (vii) Expenditure need
2	Matching grants	Provincial and local	For infrastructure development, consider: (i) Feasibility of the project (ii) Cost of the project (iii) Output or benefit to be achieved (iv) Financial and physical capacity or human resources to implement the project (v) Need and priority of the project
3	Special grants	Provincial and local	Special grants adhere to the following objectives: (i) To supply and develop basic services like education, health, drinking water, etc. (ii) To have balanced development across SNGs (iii) To develop or uplift communities or groups experiencing discrimination

Source: National Natural Resources and Fiscal Commission Act, 2017, Section 16 (1)(2).

the perspective of SNGs. Moreover, the conditionalities can appreciably reduce the autonomy of local governments to forge their development paths or shape their services to citizens.

The government is mandated to implement the recommendations of NNRFC. NNRFC's main function is to provide recommendations on the allocation of fiscal transfers to SNGs. It must heed the Constitution's call for the transparent and fair distribution of grants. This commission comprises a chair and a maximum of four members appointed by the President on the recommendation of the Constitutional Council for a tenure of 6 years. The formulation of provisions in the Constitution has unfortunately allowed for different interpretations to emerge on the role of NNRFC, whether it only makes recommendations (leaving room for Parliament to also influence transfers), or whether it can

have the last word.[41] The government needs to make clear that the technical "determination" of grants does not override the many provisions in the Constitution that describe the NNRFC role as advisory.

Constitutional provisions for IGFTs are further elaborated on in legislation. The Intergovernmental Fiscal Arrangement Act, 2017 sets out the sharing of the revenue derived from the VAT and excise duty collected from domestic production, as well as royalty incomes collected by the federal government. The act specifies the proportions to be distributed among federal, provincial, and local governments. As per the act, equalization grants are to be provided based on expenditure needs and revenue capacity of the provincial and local governments, while conditional grants are to be provided based on criteria prescribed by NNRFC. In practice—while NNRFC is under

---

41   World Bank. 2019. *Policy Note for the Federalism Transition in Nepal*. Washington, DC: World Bank.

formation—proposals for equalization grants are prepared by sector ministries, and final grant amounts are decided by the MOF.

Provincial governments are also mandated to transfer funds to local governments, but their role in the IGFT framework is not as strong as in other federations. The provinces do provide local governments with grants (Appendix 10) but do not have a free hand; their policies are shaped by NNRFC. In contrast, several federal nations give the state or provincial level a strong allocation role concerning local government (e.g., Australia, Canada, India, Pakistan, and United States). This level of government provides the bulk of the grants to its local government (Box 5), possibly supplemented by federal grants, with efforts made to coordinate the two sources of funding.

In the case of Nepal, the federal government appears to treat both the provinces and local governments as essentially similar—as levels of SNGs that are financially subordinate to the federal government—supplying both levels with substantial grants. This financial architecture (entrenched in part due to fiscal imbalance) has implications that spill beyond financing. The entire policy and planning framework of the country is affected, with local governments likely to be oriented toward the federal level rather than the provincial level. This orientation could be corrected (or balanced) to the extent that the province itself provides local government with substantial funding in areas critical to local development.

The federal government retains most of the revenue it collects (50%–70%) and shares the rest equally with the provinces and local governments. As per the IGFA Act, 2017, SNGs are eligible to receive 30% of revenue from VAT and excise duty, and 50% of the royalty from water and natural resources, mountaineering, electricity generation and distribution, and forests and minerals (Table 12). The sharing ratios are not reflective of the heavier load of service delivery responsibilities assigned to the local government.

Fiscal equalization grants to SNGs are used to close the gap between expenditure needs and revenue potential, but the equity built into the distribution formula is questioned. The grant is distributed from the federal consolidated fund based on recommendations of NNRFC. The grant is formula-based, with parameters comprising population, the total area of the respective jurisdiction, the human development index, and other development indicators. Population has been the dominant parameter, an emphasis that is questioned by some stakeholders, particularly in rural municipalities with relatively smaller populations that can translate into higher per capita costs of

---

BOX 5
Nepal Subnational Government Efforts to Increase Revenue

Municipalities raise more than half of their revenues from local sources and receive both federal and provincial transfers. However, the provincial grants are more than 10 times as large as federal grants. Federal grants are earmarked, as in the case of the gas tax fund which is dedicated to support infrastructure development for cleaner air and water and reduced greenhouse gas emissions. Most provincial government transfers are conditional grants aimed at financing specific services at levels and standards that are set by the province. Some of these standards are influenced by federal transfers to the provinces. Most provinces also provide some form of equalization grants to municipalities, and each province can define its own municipal equalization scheme, but these do not generally constitute the major component of grants.

Sourse E. Slack. 2008. *Financing Municipal Services and Infrastructure in Canada.* Presentation to EkoAkete Summit IV. Lagos, Nigeria. July.

Table 12: Mandated Formulas for Transfers of Revenue
from Federal to Subnational Governments (%)

Sr. No.	Source	Federal	Province	Local
	Taxes			
1	VAT	70	15	15
2	Excise	70	15	15
	Royalty from Natural Resources			
1	Mountaineering	50	25	25
2	Electricity	50	25	25
3	Forest	50	25	25
4	Mines and minerals	50	25	25
5	Water and other natural resources	50	25	25

Source: Intergovernmental Fiscal Arrangement (IGFA) Act, 2017.

service.[42] The revised indicators for fiscal equalization grants are provided in Table 13 and updated grant amounts are provided in Table 14.[43]

Nepal has reserved a small percentage of grants to be based on the performance of the SNGs, building on a decade of experience with performance-based grants. Performance-based grants were always a small portion of funding for SNGs. This will not change in the new framework, as Nepal is aiming to incorporate a modest incentive for performance in its equalization grants, aimed to spur achievement in governance processes as the grants were originally designed.[44] However, the government seeks to eventually orient the incentives to achievement in service delivery.[45]

In introducing performance principles, the government may need to consider whether equalization grants are the best grant type for promoting performance, given the tension between equity and performance; perhaps other grant types are more suited. It can also be argued that making the intergovernmental system function on a compliance basis is an important initial achievement that could be jeopardized by introducing more complicated components, such as performance principles.

---

[42] Institute for Integrated Development Studies (IIDS). 2020. *Fiscal Federalism in Nepal: Revenue Potential of Provincial and Local Governments and Recommendations to Enhance Own-Source Revenue Generation.*

[43] The amounts of grants for the provincial and local levels are recommended under three modalities or ways: (i) minimum amount that every SNG is entitled to receive for the year, (ii) amount recommended based on formulas, and (iii) remaining 5%, based on performance of the governments. For determining the minimum amount of the grant—in the case of the province—only two indicators (population and area) are considered with a weightage of 50% each. At the local level, only one criterion is considered: population. E.g., in FY2021, NRs25 million was given to those with a population of less than 10,000, NRs27.5 million was given to those with a population of 10,000 to 20,000, and NRs112.5 million to those with a population over 500,000. (Source: K. L. Devkota, International Center for Public Policy, George State University. 2020. Intergovernmental Fiscal Transfers in a Federal Nepal. Atlanta.) (NNRFC Introductory Book and Progress Report 2020).

[44] Based on FY2021, the performance indicators were as follows: mandated governance processes such as numbers of laws formulated; submission of budgets to corresponding legislatures in fixed date and time; status of category of expenditures like capital expenditure, recurrent expenditure, total expenditure and budget spent on the operating/administrative area; preparation and submission of statements and reports to the Government of Nepal and provincial governments (at the local level); undertaking timely final audits, and others.

[45] Report prepared for grant recommendation, for FY2021 by NNRFC.

Table 13: Updated Indicators for Fiscal Equalization Grants, Fiscal Year 2021

Sr. No.	Base/Indicators	Internal Modality Measures (Weight of Subindicators in %)	Modality/ Measures (Weight %)
1	Human Development Index[a]	–	10
2	Socioeconomic Discrimination Index[b]	–	5
3	Infrastructure Development Index	–	10
	Road Density (access to road transportation)	60	
	Facility of Electricity (access to electricity)	10	
	Facility of ICT (access to communication)	10	
	Facility of Drinking Water (access to drinking water)	10	
	Sanitation (access to toilet facilities)	10	
4	Revenue Status	–	5
5	Expenditure Need	–	70
		Total	100

ICT = information and communication technology.
Note: Numbers may not sum precisely because of rounding.
[a] Based on the Nepal Human Development Report 2014.
[b] This index comprises six sectors/dimensions including social, economic, risk created by climate change, and disasters.
Source: Government of Nepal, National Natural Resources and Fiscal Commission. 2021. Annual Report.

Table 14: Updated Amounts of Fiscal Equalization Grants, Fiscal Year 2021

Sr. No.	Fiscal Equalization Grants	Amount (NRs Billion)	% of the Total
1	Based on the formula for 7 provinces	41.02	71.24
2	Provided based on performance for 7 provinces	2.16	3.76
	Total amounts recommended to 7 provinces	57.57	100
3	Minimum amounts for local levels	24.62	26.25
4	Based on the formula for local levels	65.67	70.00
5	Performance based for local levels	3.45	3.75
6	Minimum amount (not less than) for each local level	0.025	–
	Total for 753 local levels (NRs billion)	93.74	100
	Total provinces and local levels (NRs billion)	151.31	10.26*

Note: Numbers may not sum precisely because of rounding.
*10.26% of total budget of the Government of Nepal for FY2021.
Source: Government of Nepal, National Natural Resources and Fiscal Commission. 2021. Annual Report.

Findings on Intergovernmental Transfers to SNGs

Setting aside the first year of transfers (FY2018), revenue sharing and grants have yet to show significant growth during FY2019–FY2021. SNG grants grew about 4% over this period, reaching NRs4.847 billion with a provincial share of NRs1.625 million and a local government share of NRs3.222 million. Revenue sharing and fiscal equalization grants have remained stable or grown minimally at best, whereas conditional grants have grown considerably for local governments, but have decreased at the provincial level. This trend may reflect a recognition of the relatively larger spending responsibilities of local governments.

The lack of growth in overall transfers suggests that SNGs are struggling to fulfill their newly defined mandates. This is particularly likely as their revenues have yet to show strong growth, at least on a provincial level. At the local government level, the strong shift to conditional grants suggests that the federal government is seeking to strongly direct local government spending. The shift away from fiscal equalization grants raises the question of whether the provinces and local governments are being treated equitably.

Provincial transfers to local government have been much smaller than those transferred by the federal government. In FY2021, seven provinces altogether allocated NRs27.097 billion for granting purposes to the local levels; with the highest figure by Bagmati (NRs7.243 billion) and the lowest by Gandaki (NRs2.144 billion) (Appendix 10). Based on the figures in Table 15, the federal transfer to local governments in FY2021 is about 10 times larger (NRs261.101 billion) than those provided by the provincial governments. This difference underscores that the federal level has the most influence on local government, in contrast to many federations where the formative units (provinces) play the dominant role in local government.

Grants received by SNGs during FY2019–FY2021 have stagnated and do not seem to closely follow the growth or decline of national revenues. Table 15 shows that transfers to SNGs dropped slightly from FY2018 to FY2019—most markedly for the provincial level—due to the decline of conditional grants. Yet during these 2 years, the national budget increased by 17%, suggesting that there is not a good link between national revenues and SNG grants. In some countries, the size of major grants (such as the equalization grant expected in Nepal) is tied to national revenues (Box 6). Without a fixed proportion, it is easier for the central government to shift between grants and suppress the growth of grants.

The NNRFC has cautiously applied performance-based indicators in determining the fiscal equalization grants. A 2.5% share in the fiscal equalization grant was implemented in FY2020. For FY2021, 3.75% of the provinces' fiscal equalization grant will be performance-based. It will be 3.68% for local governments. As the share of the equalization grant has slid in relative terms, the performance-based component has failed to become a significant component of the overall grant system.

Table 15: Transfers from Federal to Provincial and Local Governments (NRs billion)

Sr. No.	Heads/FYs	FY2018	FY2019	FY2020	FY2021*
A	Revenue Sharing (I+II)	0	114.24	130.89	122.14
I	Province	0	60.42	65.44	61.07
II	Local	0	53.82	65.44	61.07
B	Total SNG Grants (I+II)	232.19 0	353.12	333.67	362.60
I	Local	225.05	229.69	223.82	261.10
	Fiscal Equalization	148.63	85.20	89.95	90.05
	Conditional	76.41	109.84	123.87	161.08
	Matching	0	5.00	5.00	4.98
	Special	0	5.00	5.00	4.99
II	Province	7.14	123.43	109.85	101.50
	Fiscal Equalization	7.14	50.29	55.30	55.19
	Conditional	0	63.13	44.55	36.35
	Matching	0	5.00	5.00	4.98
	Special	0	5.00	5.00	4.98
	Sharing + Grant SNGs (A+B)	232.19	467.36	464.56	484.74

FY = fiscal year, SNG = subnational government.
Note: Numbers may not be exact due to rounding.
*Amounts are based on budget proposals or are estimated.
Sources: Government of Nepal, Ministry of Finance, and arranged by the team.

BOX 6
International Good Practice in Setting the Equalization Grants Pool

The equalization pool is often a fixed proportion of central government revenues or is determined on an ad hoc basis. Ad hoc equalization fails to provide much certainty for SNG planning. To provide some degree of stability to local governments and some degree of flexibility to the central government, it is best to establish a fixed percentage of central government revenues; this is done in countries like Indonesia, Argentina, and Colombia. Setting the proportion of equalization grants with overall government revenues ensures that SNGs do well when national revenues grow and share the loss on revenue downturns.

Source: R.M. Bird and M. Smart. 2002. Intergovernmental Fiscal Transfers: International Lessons for Developing Countries. *World Development*, 30:6, June, pp. 899–912.

Challenges in Fiscal Transfers

The intention of NNRFC to seek better performance in the use of fiscal equalization grants has been stymied by reduced revenues due to COVID-19 and faces contradictory impulses. For FY2021, NNRFC recommended that performance grants be raised to 3.8% of the total pool for equalization grants flowing to the local and provincial governments. However, the federal government declined to implement this recommendation due to the decrease in revenue collection as an impact of the COVID-19 pandemic.[46] The impact of the pandemic on Nepal's economy—and hence its revenues—is sure to wane in the coming years.

---

[46]   K.L. Devkota. 2020. Intergovernmental Fiscal Transfers in a Federal Nepal. *International Center for Public Policy Working Paper Series*, Working Paper 20–17. Atlanta: International Center for Public Policy, Andrew Young School of Policy Studies, Georgia State University.

However, in seeking to further develop the performance-based granting, the government will need to reconcile the equalization grant as an entitlement of the SNGs that delivers on the commitment to close gaps between expenditure needs and revenue capacity, with the desire to enforce a national view of SNG performance. These aims can cause tension. Performing SNGs may attract more transfer funds, but potentially at the cost of equity in resources for development and services across SNGs.

Conditional grants are being used as a means of ad hoc micromanagement of SNGs, putting off more durable mechanisms that give SNGs more discretion in discharging their functions. The mindset of the unitary state is taking some time to shift. The vertical fiscal imbalance is providing an opening for its persistence. For instance, wages for teachers and health workers have been subsumed under conditional grants, whereas the constitutional intention for conditional grants was to support infrastructure development. Exerting control through financing can become a shortcut to accountability that limits the development of frameworks that guide SNGs more gently and encourages the responsible and integrated management of SNG functions.

Federal and provincial transfers and revenue sharing have no clear connection to expenditure assignments to SNGs. The heavy reliance on conditional grants rather than equalization grants—and the lack of transparency on the proportions of revenue sharing as of 2021—underscores that there has not been a systematic effort to link the financing of SNGs to their assigned functions. A proper connection would require that the functions have better definition and costing, which is undermined by the heavy degree of concurrence in the assignment of functions. Subsequent elaboration and divisions have not yet helped in this regard.

The secretariat of NNRFC faces serious challenges in obtaining the data that support good policymaking by NNRFC. Data comes from line ministries and the Central Bureau of Statistics, but improvements in the data are needed that effectively channel the needed data from local and provincial levels to the federal level (e.g., a well-designed and executed SuTRA system should supply local financial data, whereas the provincial line ministry budget information system, the computerized government accounting system, and the Treasury Single Account in each province should provide such information for provincial governments).

Recommendations

Intergovernmental grant systems are crafted to pursue multiple objectives, but may conflict (e.g., minimizing the vertical fiscal imbalance versus ensuring horizontal equalization; allocating grants based on performance versus need; encouraging local initiative and accountability versus exerting vertical control and accountability).

The following recommendations offer directions to the state and NNRFC on improving the system while being mindful of these realities.

Any increase in the share of performance-based transfers should not undermine horizontal equity and should prioritize incentives for SNG revenue mobilization. As a means of incentivizing OSR mobilization at the subnational level, the government could consider increasing the share of performance-based transfers to SNGs through an appropriate grant (e.g., special grant rather than equalization grant). Such performance-based grants would incentivize SNGs to make the most of the discretion given to them in raising revenues through increased digitization and efficient collection. The timing of the increased performance-based grant (a more complex grant to administer) should be such that it does not complicate the initial drive to gain compliance with the requirements of the main grants.

Anchoring grant allocations for SNGs in legislation would promote certainty and accountability. Having the intergovernmental grant allocations determined and finalized as an act before the budget is finalized would give provincial and local governments more time to prepare their plans and budgets within more firm budget ceilings. The legislation could allow for some modification in the finalized budgets.

A minimum fixed portion of revenue collected by the federal government and transferred to provincial and local governments would help to avoid an increasingly severe vertical fiscal imbalance. This practice has provided countries like Indonesia with more predictability and certainty (the main block transfer is set at 26% of net national revenue).[47] This can lend stability and flexibility to the system. It would be a firmer base from which to try and reduce the vertical fiscal gap through other means such as increasing own revenues.

---

[47] B. Hofman et al. 2006. Evaluating Fiscal Equalization in Indonesia. *World Bank Policy Research Working Paper.* No. 3911. Washington, DC: World Bank.

CHAPTER VI

SUBNATIONAL BORROWING

Legal Provisions for SNGs Borrowing

The Constitution of Nepal allows all three levels of government to borrow funds to meet expenditure needs that cannot be met through regular resources. However, directly engaging in external borrowing is allowed only at the federal level. Provincial governments may borrow externally, subject to approval from the federal government.[48] Similarly, local governments may mobilize external borrowings through the federal or provincial government. With grants, the NNRFC plays a large role in making recommendations about domestic borrowing and its limits for the three levels of government. It bases its recommendations on its analysis of macroeconomic indicators. Additional details on SNG borrowing are found in the IGFA Act, 2017. For instance, the act provides for the possibility of internal loans from the federal government to SNGs.

The IGFA Act, 2017 also allows the provincial governments to issue bonds (debentures) but excludes local governments from these powers. Section 14(2) of the act only mentions the government of Nepal and the province as having the power to issue debentures. It is larger cities that are most in need of these powers, making this exclusion problematic.

Findings on SNG Borrowing

The level of borrowing in Nepal is low at all levels of government. The national government tries to chart a prudent macroeconomic course, managing to keep its outstanding public debt-to-GDP ratio at around 30% until FY2019 when it has pushed above 41%.[49] Borrowing at the subnational level also remains very low, in contrast to the strong private sector growth in credit seen in recent years. The NNRFC has set limits annually for SNG borrowing, but these are disconnected from the actual potential

---

[48] In Schedule 5, the Constitution of Nepal grants the federal government powers related to foreign grants, aid, and loans. In Schedule 6, the provincial governments are assigned powers related to the operation of banks and financial institutions in accordance with the policies of Nepal Rastra Bank (NRB), and foreign grants and assistance with the consent of the federal government.

[49] Government of Nepal. 2020. Economic Survey 2019/20.

for borrowing as of 2021.[50] SNG borrowing—derived largely from state banks—comprises only 0.85% of total municipal revenues.[51]

For FY2019, three provinces proposed to raise domestic loans in their budget estimates: Province 2 proposed NRs1 billion, Gandaki Province proposed NRs800 million, and Karnali Province proposed NRs1 billion. But none of these provinces were able to mobilize the loans. There is a lack of a strong domestic capital market, and there are not many institutions that serve the municipal credit segment except for the TDF.[52] Moreover, there are institutional and policy impediments to the development of municipal credit institutions.

As of 2021, no SNG has issued debentures, and it is not clear that they are progressing toward the use of this financing option. In part, the lack of progress reflects the larger capital market environment where even corporate bonds are uncommon. The market is exceedingly thin on both supply and demand. Short-term government debt dominates the bond market. There are few investors; treasury instruments are bought largely by banks to satisfy statutory liquidity requirements.

While higher level policy on SNG borrowing is permissive, the regulatory framework is still being developed. The government is concerned with maintaining macroeconomic stability and therefore aims to develop regulations that will safeguard that stability at the national level.

On the other hand, SNGs can benefit from accessing borrowing, accelerating the pace of infrastructure development, and aligning repayments from citizen taxes and charges with the life cycle/benefits of the infrastructure. Room should be given to SNGs and their related institutions (e.g., special purpose vehicles, public–private partnerships, an association of SNGs) to access capital through the borrowing and issuing of debentures, accompanied by the necessary regulations (in advance and after) to reduce fiscal risks and promote prudent borrowing.

Regulations should aim to empower these entities to access such funds, and open opportunities for the private capital markets to serve them adequately. Unduly restrictive frameworks can retard the growth of borrowing of SNGs. Allowing borrowing and bond issuing needs to be accompanied by a regulatory and capacity development approach that allows SNGs to take advantage of favorable policies while safeguarding against possible fiscal problems. This is evident in the case of Indonesia (Box 7), where SNGs do not borrow much and have yet to issue bonds. In the case of India (Box 8), efforts have been made to build the capacity of cities to issue bonds and attain credit ratings to attract market interest. While the number of cities that have issued bonds is small, the models for others to copy are emerging. Working on both the supply and the demand side to create a market is critical.

---

50   The borrowing limits for all levels of government have been defined as a fixed number and not a range. NNRFC has determined and recommended the borrowing limits for FY2021:

   (i)   **Federal level.** The borrowing amount should not be more than 5% of the GDP of the country.

   (ii)   **Province level.** The borrowing amount should not be more than 12% of internal revenue (shared revenue plus OSR) amount mobilized by the province.

   (iii) **Local level.** The borrowing amount should not be more than 12% of internal revenue amounts collected at the local level.

   For FY2019 and FY2020, the limit for the federal government was 5% of the GDP and for provinces and local levels it was restricted to 10% of the internal revenue.

51   Needs Assessment, Costing, and Financing Strategy for Sustainable Development Goals.

52   The TDF is generally provided with grants from the federal government and loans or grants from multilateral development banks and aid agencies. It uses these funds to provide blended products to local government and to other local organizations.

BOX 7
Borrowing and Issuing Bonds in Regional Governments of Indonesia

After years of accruing arrears on central government loans, RGs (provinces and districts/cities) can now only borrow if they meet strict conditions (e.g., RG debt should not exceed 75% of the previous year's budget revenues and the debt service ratio to revenue is capped at 40%; arrears must be resolved). RGs have begun to borrow again, but the level is still modest. Since 2004, RGs can also raise domestic bonds, with the permission of the Ministry of Finance and a clean audit from the state auditor. The relatively shallow capital market, low creditworthiness, and public financial management capacity of the RGs—and a requirement to link bonds to specific projects—have made RGs unable and unwilling to take advantage of this option.

Source: ADB. 2020. *Technical Assistance Completion Report: Indonesia—Strengthening the Local Government Bond Market.* Manila.

BOX 8
Cities Supported in Bond Issuance in India

An amendment was made in the Income Act of 1961 to grant municipalities the right to issue tax-free bonds. A few municipal councils and corporations used this mechanism to raise finance (with their state government's approval) through both taxable and tax-free bonds. A state pooled finance development fund scheme has been established by the Ministry of Urban Development to provide credit enhancement to cities wishing to access the bond market. Cities are scrutinized through a mandatory rating system when the issue maturity is greater than 18 months. Nine cities have issued bonds so far.

Source: A.C. Gulankar. 2020. Lucknow Is the Ninth Indian City to Raise Money through Municipal Bonds. *The Federal.* 6 December.

The restructuring of the TDF promises to be supportive of a municipal capital market. The TDF has been providing blended finance to SNGs since its establishment in 1997, with the loan–grant composition depending on the nature of the projects; the most economic combines 90% loan from the TDF with a 10% contribution to the project. The new legislation seeks to turn the TDF around after its performance slumped to an overall loan recovery rate of approximately 65%.[53] The strategic plan 2020 calls for the development of the municipal capital market by FY2024.[54] The revamped TDF will be renamed and will serve both provincial and local government (municipal) levels. It will continue to mobilize domestic and foreign assistance to channel

financing to SNGs but will expand its sources of financing to include capital markets. In cooperation with United Nations Capital Development Fund, the TDF is seeking to develop a credit profile for itself and selected municipalities, leading to a rating of the TDF and municipalities through an independent rating agency. Five municipalities have completed the work of credit assessment as part of this cooperation.

Challenges in Developing SNG Borrowing

The restructuring of the TDF will require substantial capacity development to enable it to expand its financing sources and provide better products to SNGs. Since it was founded in 1989, the TDF has received loans, grants, and technical assistance from ADB, the World Bank, the German state-owned development bank (KfW), and GIZ (the Deutsche Gesellschaft für Internationale Zusammenarbeit). But funding

---

[53] ADB. 2012. *Technical Assistance Consultant's Report: Nepal—Strengthening the Town Development Fund Capacity for Public–Private Partnership (Financed by the Technical Assistance Special Fund).* Manila.

[54] Government of Nepal, Town Development Fund. 2020. *Business Plan FY 2020/21–2023/2024 (2077/78–2080/81): Business Plan for transforming TDF into Urban Infrastructure Development Corporation (UIDC).* Kathmandu.

sources need to be expanded to include private placements of equity and debt (e.g., bonds). This expansion will be challenging. With a larger balance sheet, the TDF must work with SNGs to identify more bankable transactions and seek to attain a much higher loan recovery rate of 95% or better.

Clarifying the access of local government to bond issuing may require an amendment to the IGFA Act, 2017. This will be challenging as there is already a backlog of legal instruments that must be prepared to complete or refine the legal framework for SNGs. Moreover, the legislative clarification must be backed up by debt mobilization guidelines that enable SNGs to prepare themselves adequately and allow them to manage debt (including bonds) professionally. SNGs will need to increase their capacity to identify and design quality investment plans, identify and mitigate fiduciary risks, and build trust in the system by enhancing transparency and accountability (e.g., by making their financial reports—including debt positions—more accessible). This capacity development is more urgent than changing the IGFA Act, 2017, which can be done later as the readiness to borrow increases.

Recommendations

The generally permissive framework for SNG borrowing requires some clarification, implementing guidelines, and institutional elaboration. In particular, the mandate for issuing debentures and bonds by local governments needs to be explicitly codified in law. National SNG guidelines on managing debt need to be provided to SNGs to develop policies and debt managing units that adhere to the national framework. Particularly at the provincial level, new or more suitable organizational units should be established for effective debt management, e.g., a debt management office.

Greater access to SNG borrowing needs to be facilitated, but it should be preceded by efforts to make SNGs more bankable. Facilitating access will require making the private banking sector more familiar with SNGs and expanding the reach of financial intermediaries like the TDF. A suggested approach is the creation of desk offices of the TDF for each of the seven provinces. This would allow the TDF to better respond to SNG requests for project-based capital financing. Further reforms include the creation of provincial-level TDFs following the framework of the federal model. Increased capacity development of SNGs to make good use of borrowing is even more urgent, in project planning and management, mitigating fiduciary risks, and building trust in the system by enhancing transparency and accountability.

It will be important to track SNG debt at a national level to ensure there will be transparency and macroeconomic vigilance. An important way to work toward this vigilance will be to expand the use of the debt operations and management system to include domestic borrowings by SNGs. This would allow for better management of public debt and would lead to a "single source of truth" regarding public debt of the various tiers of governments in Nepal.

CHAPTER VII

CONCLUSIONS AND LESSONS FROM NEPAL'S JOURNEY TOWARD FISCAL FEDERALISM

Nepal is making headway in its efforts to establish a federal system of governance. It has an aspirational Constitution that is favorable to a devolved form of governance. It has elaborated key provisions of the Constitution in legislation, and it has implemented many important elements of what is understood to be "fiscal decentralization." Considerable resources have been directed to SNGs and capacity development efforts are evident. However, the past 5 years have proven to be insufficient to realize the full intent of the new Constitution, particularly as efforts have not been guided by a reform and capacity development road map.

The transition to a federal system that is meaningfully decentralized is vast and calls for persistent efforts to assess and develop capacity for reform design and implementation. This is true for attaining fiscal federalism and other core commitments in the new Constitution. The capacity to realize the lofty provisions of the new Constitution is still emerging in Nepal and will require a heavy orientation to capacity development at all levels of government. The issue of capacity has been recognized (e.g., in the MOFAGA 2019

assessment), but capacities need to be assessed periodically—reflecting the priority reforms anticipated or underway—with adjustments in the strategies employed to meet capacity needs based on how well capacity development interventions have worked.[55]

Capacity assessments should be ongoing commitments of key institutions at all levels, with a broad view encompassing individual, organizational, and system-level needs.[56] In this respect, development partner support can be very helpful. For instance, the 2015 public expenditure and financial accountability review—with its subnational component—was an important aid to further program design for initiatives oriented to SNGs; another such review focused on SNGs would be timely and useful given the established baseline.[57]

The overall reform load needs to focus on the federal and SNG levels in a sequential manner. Matching reform load with capacity can be done by prioritizing reforms, arrived at through sound consultation. The partial implementation and challenges faced in the reforms initiated as of 2021 are suggestive of

[55] Georgia State University, Andrew Young School of Public Policy, and the Nepal Administrative Staff College. 2019. *Capacity Needs Assessment for the Transition to Federalism. Sponsored by the Government of Nepal, Ministry of Federal Affairs and General Administration,* World Bank Group, and United Nations Development Programme (UNDP).

[56] UNDP. 2009. *Capacity Development: A UNDP Primer.*

[57] Independent Evaluation Department. 2019. *Validation Report—Nepal: Strengthening Public Management Program.* Manila: ADB.

a government that is struggling to undertake numerous and weighty reforms simultaneously. It is important to show some initial success of federalism and to maintain citizen support and the momentum of reforms. This means matching the reform load to the emerging capacities of key actors. The political development of SNGs was suppressed for many years during the period of internal conflict; local elections only took place in 2017 following a 20-year gap. All SNGs are new or recombined in their constituent populations and previous structures. Civil servants are still being moved about, and many vacancies are found at all levels, leading to a lack of skills required for many of the ongoing and anticipated reforms and improvements. Capacity is being largely absorbed in adjusting even to these aspects of restructuring.

Yet many other reforms are also underway or being proposed. While each additional reform viewed on its own may seem well-calibrated to existing capacities, in sum the reform agenda may simply overwhelm government and stakeholder capacity. This could result in pilots or national initiatives that—even when supported by development partners—fail to scale up or mature. Gaining stakeholder consensus on the most crucial reform is critical. As in other countries (e.g., public financial management reforms supported in Cambodia by many development partners), the coordinating or consultative platforms should yield phased sets of mutually reinforcing and feasible reforms. For instance, full MTEF implementation would be placed farther down the road, giving SNGs a chance to first build a good financial data and reporting system that links to vertical and social accountability.

Priority could go to building up the capacity of SNGs to spend efficiently given the challenges faced in realizing budgets. Changes in the SNG borrowing framework and supply-oriented support could also yield precedence to the broad governance improvements that would make SNGs more bankable. Performance-based grants could follow basic compliance in implementing grant implementation and reporting requirements.

Fiscal federalism and decentralization require platforms that address system-wide reforms that enhance the coordination and assessment of reforms. The institutional self-assessment process established for local government by MOFAGA (Local Government Institutional Self-Assessment: LISA) is valuable but needs to be embedded in a system of communication and negotiation that also addresses national and provincial policy framework issues. For example, improving budget execution rates and quality of expenditures is a local government challenge, but it also needs earlier notice of—and more stable—revenue sharing and intergovernmental grant allocations; these are systemic issues under the control of the federal government. Similarly, provincial and local governments can build up their debt management units, but the revamped TDF needs to offer more relevant products and strong support to SNGs to prepare bankable projects.

The new coordination mechanisms need to be made workable, providing platforms for shaping the transition to federalism and its consolidation. The Government of Nepal recently passed the Federation, Province and Local Level (Coordination and Interrelationship) Act, 2020 (2077). This act provides principles of management, consultation, and dispute resolution that guide the implementation of the functional assignment placed in the Constitution. It provides details on the constitutionally established National Coordination Council and Provincial Coordination Councils. For both councils, it provides for representation from rural and municipal local governments.

By feeding the experiences back to provincial and national policymakers, these new platforms can help to shape policies that have legitimacy and practicality. These coordination platforms could give rise to practical arrangements on concurrent functions that—with lessons of experience—can eventually be embedded in revised constitutional schedules and legislation. Great care should be taken to ensure that these bodies can serve to redress grievances, and if they are not able to do so, establish separate mechanisms in this regard. The timely and appropriate handling of grievances will improve the coordination between the three tiers of government, and transparency and accountability on key pillars of fiscal federalism (e.g., transfers to SNGs).

While federalism is centralized in practice, there is still room to strengthen the role of provinces in guiding and supporting local governments. There is an opportunity to relieve the federal government of some of the load in these respects while tailoring the empowerment of local government to specific circumstances that are more discernible and actionable because of the scale of the province. Provinces should be supported to build their capacity to engage with local government to apply national systems where appropriate but otherwise find provincial and local solutions. Before federalism, the Local Governance and Community Development Programme (2008–2016) was the flagship nationwide program on local governance.

The successor program—the Provincial and Local Governance Support Program (2020–2023)—envisages the establishment of provincial centers for good governance as key service providers for local government capacity building and for supporting the establishment of effective and responsive provincial governance processes. Provincially shaped programs—with direct development partner support—could provide a tailored and innovation-rich approach to ways of supporting SNG development. However, this will require establishing functioning mechanisms of communication and collaboration between the municipalities and the provinces.

COVID-19 highlights the need for a more robust federal system. The increase in demand for service delivery and relief efforts during the pandemic tested the nascent federal system and unraveled weaknesses across different levels of the government. This underscores the urgency to enstablish more robust intergovernmental relations. Good coordination would make it easier to sort roles that are insufficiently developed in the Constitution or legislation. When the health threat recedes, the government will need to show the same zeal shown in combatting the pandemic by committing to a robust fiscal decentralization framework and capacity development of SNGs.

Nepal offers reform lessons that may be relevant to policymakers in other countries contemplating a transition to fiscal decentralization. Key lessons that can be drawn from the relatively early stages of the transition in Nepal include the following:

(i)   It takes time to bring about and institutionalize new policies, legal frameworks, and practices. Time is needed to change mindsets, and broad stakeholder support must be maintained.

(ii)   A reform road map—embedded in a communication strategy—is needed from the start to manage a deep set of political and administrative reforms.

(iii) It is important to show some initial success on issues that matter to citizens to maintain support and momentum for reforms. This approach calls for phased reforms that do not overwhelm the capacities of key actors.

(iv)   Pursuing fiscal decentralization means ensuring that there is sufficient discretion given to SNGs to reflect the intentions of the country's constitution, in legislation that accords with the constitutional provisions, and capacity development that allows SNGs to make full use of their new powers.

(v)   As SNGs are given more resources and discretion, it becomes more important to hold SNGs accountable. This means that intergovernmental roles and assigned functions need to be well demarcated to allow citizens to know who is responsible, with any concurrence being purposeful and its operational mechanism well understood.

(vi)   Shaping a governance system that gives both discretion and accountability to SNGs means bringing stakeholders together to give it shape and to make refinements as lessons of implementation emerge. Coordination mechanisms that are workable and trusted are essential to maintain the goodwill of key stakeholders as they work together to shape their relationships in a process that respects their distinct and interdependent roles.

APPENDIXES

Appendix 1: Constitutional Distribution of Expenditure Rights to Subnational Governments

Expenditure Function	Provinces (Schedule 6)	Local Level (Schedule 8)	Concurrent Rights (Schedule 9) Federal, Provincial and Local Level
Education	Provincial level universities, higher education, and libraries	Basic and secondary education	Education
Public Health	Health services	Basic health and sanitation; management of senior citizens, people with disability	Health
Transportation Infrastructure	Provincial highways, Infrastructure management, transportation	Local roads, rural roads, agriculture roads	–
Agriculture	Agriculture and livestock development, irrigation projects	Irrigation; management, operation, and control of agriculture extension	Agriculture
Law and Order	Provincial police administration as well as law and order, Provincial investigation Bureau	Municipal Police	–
Conservation of Environment and Natural Resources	Management of national forest, water resources, and ecology within the province; exploration and management of mines	Conservation of watershed, wetland, wildlife, mines, and minerals	Forest, wildlife, birds, water use, environment, ecology and biodiversity; Conservation of watershed, wetland, wildlife, mines, and minerals
Administration	Provincial civil service and other government services, land management, record-keeping of the land	Local statistics and record keeping, management of local records	–
Water and Electricity	Provincial level electricity, drinking water	Drinking water, small electricity projects, alternative energy	–
Heritage Conservation	Protection and use of language, culture, script, fine arts, and religion; museums	Preservation and development of language, culture, and fine arts	Archaeology, ancient monuments, and museums
Industries	Factories, industrialization, and business	–	–

Appendix 2: Budget for Provincial Governments from FY2018 to FY2021 (NRs billion)

FY		Provinces Heads	1	2	Bagmati	Gandaki	Lumbini	Karnali	Sudur Pashchim	Total (7 Provinces)
2018	Budget	Recurrent	0.66	0.43	0.45	0.58	0.44	0.43	0.42	3.44
		Capital	0.35	0.59	0.57	0.44	0.58	0.58	0.60	3.73
		Financing	–	–	–	–	–	–	–	–
		Total Budget	1.02	1.02	1.02	1.02	1.02	1.02	1.02	7.17
	Actual	Recurrent	0.43	0.26	0.14	0.09	0.12	0.12	0.16	1.35
		Capital	0.21	0.25	0.87	0.14	0.06	0.11	0.09	1.76
		Financing	–	–	–	–	–	–	–	–
		Total Exp	0.65	0.52	1.02	0.24	0.19	0.23	0.25	3.12
		Total Exp (%)	0.63	0.51	0.99	0.23	0.18	0.23	0.25	0.43
2019	Budget	Recurrent	14.92	14.47	12.87	8.11	–	7.02	13.35	70.77
		Capital	23.57	15.31	21.75	15.90	–	21.25	11.71	109.51
		Financing	–	–	–	–	–	40.00	–	40
		Total Budget	38.49	29.78	34.63	24.02	25.37	28.28	25.06	205.65
	Actual	Recurrent	9.76	6.62	11.09	5.21	6.86	4.60	6.93	51.09
		Capital	11.43	8.46	9.55	8.71	10.17	5.36	7.23	60.94
		Financing	–	–	–	–	–	0.04	–	0.04
		Total Exp	21.20	15.09	20.65	13.92	17.03	10.01	14.16	112.08
		Total Exp (%)	0.55	0.50	0.59	0.57	0.67	0.35	0.56	0.54
2020	Budget	Recurrent	18.54	19.26	24.46	12.28	17.84	13.05	14.69	120.15
		Capital	23.57	19.26	22.83	19.84	18.57	21.29	13.06	138.46
		Financing	–	–	–	–	–	–	–	–
		Total Budget	42.12	38.52	47.30	32.13	36.41	34.35	27.76	258.62
	Actual	Recurrent	4.32	2.72	3.94	2.61	5.85	2.15	2.84	24.45.
		Capital	7.45	1.03	4.13	5.38	5.68	1.74	2.32	27.76
		Financing	–	–	–	–	–	–	–	–
		Total Exp	11.78	3.75	8.07	7.99	11.54	3.90	5.16	52.22
		Total Exp (%)	0.27	0.09	0.17	0.24	0.31	0.11	0.18	20
2021	Budget	Recurrent	18.93	15.42	26.28	14.34	17.73	14.67	16.32	123.71
		Capital	21.92	17.97	25.14	19.99	18.61	19.06	16.75	13,9.49
		Financing	–	–	–	0.15	–	–	0.23.00	0.38
		Total Budget	40.85	33.40	51.42	34.49	36.35	33.74	33.31	263.58

FY = fiscal year.

Appendix 3: Timeline of Annual Federal Budget

SN	Stage of Action	Res. Agency	Time Frame	Sources/Laws
1	Initiation of annual budget preparation	Line Ministries	*Magh* first week (second week Jan)	Sec.7, FPFA Act
2	Resource estimation and determination of expenditure amounts for the coming 3 years	NPC	*Magh* 15 (tentatively 29 Jan)	Sec.8, FPFA Act
3	Forwarding of budget ceiling rand guidelines to line ministries and other concerned agencies	NPC	End of *Magh* (tentatively 14 Feb)	Sec.8, FPFA Act
4	Receiving of Budget Ceiling and Guidelines NPC	Line Ministries/Centers	End of *Magh* (tentatively 14 Feb)	Sec.8, FPFA Act
5	Providing particulars of the estimated source of fiscal equalization grants and revenue sharing to be allocated to the provincial and local levels by the Government of Nepal in the next fiscal year.	Ministry of Finance	End of *Falgun* (tentatively 15 Mar)	Sec.18, IGFM Act,
6	Presentation of principles and priorities of budget in Federal Parliament	Federal Finance Minster	At least 15 days before the submission of budget (tentatively last week of *Baisakh*/April)	FPFA Act Sec.11
7	Submission of presentation of principles and priorities of budget in Joint Meeting of two houses of Federal Parliament	Federal Finance Minster	At least 15 days before submission of the Budget (Tentatively last week of *Baisakh* /April)	Article 119, The Constitution FPFA Act Sec.11 and Sec 21, IGFM Act
8	Monitoring and evaluation of Annual Budget Reports	Line Ministries and Responsible Cost Centers	Monthly and trimester basis	FPFA Act Sec.23
9	Preparing and forwarding the trimester Budget Progress Report	Line Ministries	15 days before the date of publishing the integrated report by the Ministry of Finance	FPFA Act Sec.23
10	Publishing Integrated Budget Progress Review Reports	Ministry of Finance	Half-yearly and annually	FPFA Act Sec.23
11	Publishing Half Year Progress Report	Ministry of Finance	By end of *Magh* (tentatively 14 Feb)	FPFA Act Sec.23
12	Publishing Annual Progress Report	Ministry of Finance	By end of Kartik/4 months after completion of fiscal year	FPFA Act Sec.23, Sec.30, IGFM Act
13	Submission of Integrated Consolidated Financial Statement of Federal Accounting to the Auditor General	FCGO/Ministry of Finance		FPFA Act Sec.29
14	Preparation of an Integrated Financial Statement including federal, provincial, and local level financial statements	Government of Nepal	By end of *Paush* next fiscal year *Magh* (tentatively 14 Dec)	Sec.30, IGFM Act
15	Disseminating financial statements/reports through digital or other mediums prepared under the FPFA Act		By 7 days, from the last date defined for the preparation of statements/report	FPFA Act Sec.56

Baisakh = first month of the Nepalese Calendar, *Falgun* = eleventh month of the Nepalese calendar, FCGO = Financial Comptroller General Office, FPFA = Fiscal Procedures and Financial Accountability, IGFM = Intergovernmental Fiscal Management, Kartik = seventh month of the Nepalese calendar, *Magh* = tenth month of the Nepalese Calendar, NPC = National Planning Commission, *Paush* = ninth month of the Nepalese calendar

Appendix 4: Timeline of Annual Provincial Budget

SN	Stage of Action	Res. Agency	Time Frame	Sources/Laws
1	Analysis of macroeconomic projection	MOEAP	By end of *Paush* (tentatively 14 Dec)	Prov. Planning Guideline
2	Submission of the particulars related to budget with revenue and expenditure projection for next FY to Government of Nepal	MOEAP	By end of *Paush* (tentatively 14 Dec)	Sec.18, IGFM Act
3	Determination of Expenditure Ceiling and Estimation of Resources	MOEAP	By end of *Magh* (tentatively 14 Jan)	Prov. Financial Procedure Regulation (*Karnali*) Lumbini
4	Receipt of Budget Ceiling and Guidelines from the Government of Nepal	MOEAP	End of *Falgun* (tentatively March 15)	Sec.18, IGFM Act
4	Providing particulars of estimated source of fiscal equalization grants and revenue sharing to be allocated to the local level by the provincial and federal government in the next fiscal year	MOEAP	By *Chaitra* 15 (tentatively 1 Mar)	Sec.18, IGFM Act
5	Forwarding of Budget Ceiling Receipt and Guidelines to line ministries and other agencies	PPC	By *Chaitra* 20	Provincial Plan and Budget Model Guideline, NPC
6	Submission of Statement of Budget with an update on current fiscal year (up to end of Falgun) to the MOEAP	Provincial Line Ministries	By end of *Chaitra*	(Rule 32, PFP Regulation (*Bagmati*)
6	Submission of Annual Budget to PPC and MOEAP	Provincial Line Ministries	By *Baisakh* 10	Provincial Plan and Budget Model Guideline, NPC
7	Finalization of Budget	MEAP	By *Baisakh* 15	Provincial Plan and Budget Model Guideline, NPC
8	Approval of Annual Program by PPC	PPC	By *Baisakh* 25	Provincial Plan and Budget Model Guideline, NPC
6	Presentation of principles and priorities of budget in Federal Parliament	Federal Finance Minster	At least 1 month before the submission of Budget (tentatively last week of *Baisakh*/April)	Financial Procedure Act (Section 9, Province 5)
10	Monitoring and evaluation of Annual Budget Reports	Provincial Line Ministries	Monthly and trimester basis	
11	Preparing and forwarding the trimester Budget Progress Report	Provincial Line Ministries	15 days before date of publishing the integrated report by the MOEAP	
12	Publishing Integrated Budget Progress Review Reports	MOEAP	Half-yearly and annually	
11	Publishing Half Year Progress Report	MOEAP	By end of *Magh* (tentatively 14 Feb)	To be defined*
12	Publishing Annual Progress Report	MOEAP	By end of Kartik/4 months after completion of fiscal year	Sec.30, IGFM Act
13	Submission of periodic statements of income and expenditures including local level information to the Federal Ministry of Finance	MOEAP	Within 15 days from the date of completion of that period	Sec.32, IGFM Act

Continued on next page

Appendix 4 Continued

SN	Stage of Action	Res. Agency	Time Frame	Sources/Laws
14	Submission of Financial Statement of Accounting to the MOEAP and Provincial Accounting Comptroller Office and Office of the Auditor General	Line Ministry/cost centers	By end of Kartik of next fiscal year	Rule 86, PFP Regulation (*Bagmati*)
15	Preparation of an integrated Financial Statement of Province including provincial and local level financial statements to the FCGO and the Office of the Auditor General	Office of Provincial Accounting Comptroller	By end of *Mangshir* of next fiscal year	Rule 86, PFP Regulation (*Bagmati*), Province 2, Province 5

Asadh = third month of the Nepalese calendar, Baisakh = first month of the Nepalese calendar, Chaitra = 12th month of the Nepalese calendar, Falgun = 11th month of the Nepalese calendar, FCGO = Financial Comptroller General Office, IGFM = Intergovernmental Fiscal Management, Kartik = seventh month of the Nepalese calendar, Magh = 10th month of the Nepalese calendar, Mangshir = eighth month of the Nepalese calendar, MOEAP = Ministry of Economic Affairs and Planning, NPC = National Planning Commission, Paush = ninth month of the Nepalese calendar, PFP = Provincial Financial Procedures, PPC = Provincial Planning Commission, Shrawan = fourth month of the Nepalese calendar.

* Half-yearly and annual report to be published within 2 months of completion of fiscal years (Financial Procedure Act, 2017 (2074), Province 5, Section 20).

Appendix 5: Timeline of Annual Local Budget

SN	Stage of Action	Res. Agency	Time Frame	Sources/Laws
1	Submission of revenue projection to Local Executive	Revenue Consultative Committee	*Paush* 15 (tentatively 1 Dec)	LGO Act/ Planning Guideline/MOFAGA
2	Submission of the particulars related to budget with revenue and expenditure projection for next FY to the Government of Nepal	Local level Executive	by End of *Paush* (tentatively 14 Dec)	Sec.18, IGFM Act/LGO Act
3	Receipt of budget ceilings and guidelines on fiscal transfer from the Government of Nepal	Local level Executive	By end of *Falgun*	Sec.18, IGFM Act/LGO Act/ Local level Budget Formulation Guideline/ MOFAGA
4	Receipt of budget ceilings and guidelines on fiscal transfer from the province	Local level Executive	By end of *Chaitra*	Sec.18, IGFM Act/LGO Act/ Local level Budget Formulation Guideline/ MOFAGA
5	Determination/estimation of resources and budget ceiling	Budget Ceiling Determining Committee	By *Baisakh* 10	Local level Budget Formulation Guideline/ MOFAGA
6	Providing budget ceiling to committees and thematic divisions	Chief of Local level/Chief Administrative Officer/ Executive	By *Baisakh* 15	Local level Budget Formulation Guideline/ MOFAGA
7	Prioritizing ward-level program formulation	Chief of local level/Chief Administrative Officer/ Executive	By *Jestha* 15	Local level Budget Formulation Guideline/ MOFAGA
8	Formulation of the integrated proposed budget for the local level for the following FY	Departments	By end of *Jestha*	Local level Budget Formulation Guideline/ MOFAGA
9	Approval of budget from the local executive	Local Executive	By *Ashadh* 5	Local level Budget Formulation Guideline/ MOFAGA
10	Submission of budget estimation with MTEF to the Local Assembly/Council	Local Executive	By Ashadh 10	Sec.21, IGFM Act, Local level Budget Formulation Guideline/MOFAGA

Continued on next page

Appendix 5   Continued

SN	Stage of Action	Res. Agency	Time Frame	Sources/Laws
11	Obtaining approval from local-level assembly on the budget	Local Assembly/Council	By end of Ashadh	Local level Budget Formulation Guideline/ MOFAGA
12	Publication of the budget for the following FY	Local Executive	By *Shrawan* 15 of next fiscal year	Local level Budget Formulation Guideline/ MOFAGA

Asadh = third month of the Nepalese calendar, *Baisakh* = first month of the Nepalese Calendar, *Chaitra* = 12th month in the Nepalese calendar, *Falgun* = 11th month of the Nepalese calendar, FY = fiscal year, IGFM = Intergovernmental Fiscal Management, LGO = Local Government Operation, *Jestha* = second month of the Nepalese calendar, MOFAGA = Ministry of Federal Affairs and General Administration, MTEF = medium-term expenditure framework, *Shrawan* = fourth month of the Nepalese calendar.

Appendix 6: Revenue Rights Listed Commonly in More than one Schedule

Revenue Rights Listed in the Exclusive Power of Both Provincial and Local Levels	Revenue Rights Listed in the Exclusive Power of All Three Levels of Government
Vehicle tax	Service charge and fee
Entertainment tax	Penalty
Advertisement tax	Tourism fee
House and land registration fee	
Service charge and fee	
Penalty	
Tourism fee	

Appendix 7: Provincial Revenues
(NRs million)

Fiscal Year	Province	1	2	Bagmati	Gandaki	Lumbini	Karnali	Sudur Pashchim	Remarks
2018 (Actual)	Own Source Revenue	–	–	–	–	–	–	–	Not collected
	Revenue Sharing	–	–	–	–	–	–	–	Not collected
	Loan	–	–	–	–	–	–	–	No borrowings
	Grant	102.05	102.05	102.05	102.05	102.05	102.05	102.05	Lump-sum grant was provided
	Deficit								
	Opening Cash Balance	–	–	–	–	–	–	–	
2019 (Actual)	Own Source Revenue	934.70	896.02	1125.91	333.51	316.82	251.57	77.95	
	Revenue Sharing	151.17		738.86	609.93	701.85	484.92	581.07	
	Loan	–	–	–	–	–	–	–	
	Grant	1094.63	1496.46	1512.57	1282.23	1725.32	1629.78	1519.23	
	Deficit	–	–	–	–	–	–	–	
	Total Incomes	2180.50	2392.48	3377.34	2225.67	2743.99	2366.27	2178.25	
2020 (Estimates)	Own Source Revenue	401.70	421.33	1189.30	618.85	489.40	722.28	48.65	
	Revenue Sharing	1027.97	1043	1060.19	520.25	991.23	–	798.72	
	Loan	–	–	–	198	–	75	–	
	Grant	2120.74	1617.74	1806.13	1396.38	1661.05	1693.32	1450.30	
	Deficit	–	–	–	–	–	–	–	
	From Cash Balance	661.63	770.5	675.17	480	500	894.74	478.53	
	Total Estimates	4,212.04	3,852.57	4,730.79	3,213.48	3,641.68	3,385.34	2,776.20	

Continued on next page

Appendix 7 *Continued*

Fiscal Year	Province	1	2	Bagmati	Gandaki	Lumbini	Karnali	Sudur Pashchim	Remarks
	Own Source Revenue	961.68	161.74	1,717.30	359.75	273.83	769.63	37.70	
	Revenue Sharing	1,112.93	1,062.54	1,188.46	888.47	1,152.52	–	787.36	
	Loan	–	–	–	–				
2021	Grant	1,511.38	1,340.59	1,486.98	1,335.99	1,414.4	1,485.41	1,423.71	
	Deficit	500	84	–	237.98	–	–	–	
	Opening Cash Balance	–	691.22	750	700	794.5	1,119.09	1,059.36	
	Total Estimates	4,085.99	3,340.09	5,142.74	3,522.19	3,635.25	3,374.13	3,308.13	

Sources: Provincial offices of the Accounting Comptroller, Ministry of Economic Affairs and Planning, Financial Comptroller General Office/Ministry of Finance, Ministry of Federal Affairs and General Administration, Office of the Auditor General.
Note: For FY2018, a lump-sum amount was provided by the Government of Nepal and none of the provinces collected any own source revenue.

Apart from the reform measures mentioned in Appendix 6, reforms have also been implemented to the various taxes assigned to the SNGs. The reform initiatives specific to certain taxes assigned to the SNGs and the rationale behind the same have been summarized as follows.

(i) **Vehicle Tax.** A tax on vehicles that affects the movement of people, goods, and services. This tax was levied by the federal government before the new Constitution (2015). As per the 2015 Constitution, vehicle tax is one of nine taxes that have been allocated to subnational governments. Both provincial and local governments are to levy the vehicle tax. The rates are to be fixed on a specific basis depending upon the type of vehicle and the purpose of use (personal or commercial). The Local Government Operation Act, 2017 assigns motor vehicle tax to be levied by the provincial governments since taxes on motorized vehicles (as opposed to vehicles with limited mobility) are more efficient when levied at the higher level of the SNG. According to the Intergovernmental Fiscal Management Act, 2017 (Schedules 3, 5), the motor vehicle tax rate is determined by the province at both provincial and local levels and the province collects the taxes. While the province retains 60% of the tax collected, the remaining 40% is to be divided among the local levels on the basis and criteria determined by NNRFC and deposited to a local consolidated fund. For vehicles with limited mobility like tanga (horse cart), rickshaws, auto-rickshaws, and electric rickshaws, the local level will determine the tax rate, collect the tax, and retain it. For this purpose, the provinces have not formulated separate vehicle tax acts; tax rates are incorporated under the annual Finance Act based on the Province Vehicle and Transportation Act, 2018 (2075). This act defines the vehicle tax, categories of vehicles including local vehicles, and the role of the tax officer. As per the finance acts, the other fees like vehicle driving licenses are deposited in the provincial consolidated fund (Province Finance Acts, 2019 and 2020, Bagmati Pradesh).

(ii) **Agricultural Income Tax.** Under the new Constitution of 2015, agricultural income tax has been assigned to the provincial governments. Like many other countries, Nepal has underexploited this tax base for various political considerations and the cyclical nature of agricultural income which is vulnerable to output and price cycles. The government provides subsidized inputs, training programs, and advisory services to the farmers. The costs incurred in providing these ultimately help in generating agricultural income for the farmers. Considering the benefit principle, this income can be taxed, although the benefit principle is hardly ever applied in practice. Exemptions could be provided to poor and marginalized farmers, in case of crop failures and subsistence agricultural activities. Except for Bagmati Province and Province 6, no other province has introduced agricultural income tax. Bagmati Province levied a tax on agricultural income for the first time on a voluntary declaration basis. Lumbini Province has imposed a tax on agricultural income, based on net income, and the rate of tax ranges from 2% to 10% (Finance Act, 2020, Province 5). However, the process for the collection of tax is yet to be formulated.

(iii) **Entertainment Tax.** This can be in the form of entrance fees for entertainment in cinemas, video halls, and cultural show halls, and is permitted within the jurisdiction or taxes levied on circus and magic shows, video, cable, etc. that are used for commercial purposes. Taxes are the concurrent rights of the provincial and local governments. They are collected by the local government which keeps 60% of the divisible amount and the remaining 40% goes to the provincial government. Citizens of a jurisdiction largely benefit from entertainment, although entertainment services can also be equally enjoyed by visitors from other jurisdictions. On the other hand, the relevant cost incurred by the government for entertainment may relate only to the maintenance of general law and order which is a public good, the benefit of which is shared not only by consumers of the specific entertainment service but also by all citizens of the jurisdiction and visitors. Therefore, the tax revenue should ideally be shared between the local and provincial governments. Lumbini Province has prepared the Entertainment Tax Rule, 2018 (2076) and the tax rates are defined by Province Finance Act. The tax collection and monitoring are done at the local level. The local government shares 40% of the tax collected with the provincial government and the same is deposited in the provincial consolidated fund.

(iv) **Advertisement Tax.** This is a concurrent right of the provincial government and local governments, as the corresponding subject is mentioned in Schedules 6 and 8 of the Constitution. The local governments levy tax on advertisements in the form of signboards, stalls, globe boards, etc. that are placed at junctions and public places under their respective jurisdiction, and it is shared between the local government and the provincial government in the ratio of 60:40. The benefits from advertisements are largely commercial as they increase the profits of suppliers who advertise their goods and services. The costs to the government are in maintaining the public roads and sites that are used to put up advertisements. Since it is difficult to measure the value of benefits derived, the benefit principle cannot be applied here. The revenues earned should be added to the divisible tax pool. Lumbini Province has prepared Advertisement Tax Rule, 2018 (2075) and the tax rates are defined by the Province Finance Act. The tax collection and monitoring and supervision of the tax are at the local level. About 40% of the tax collected by the local government is shared with the provincial government and deposited in the provincial consolidated fund.

Appendix 9: Model Acts and Rules Formulated by the Government of Nepal

Sl. No.	Model Act / Rules	Formulated by
1	Province and Local Finance Act (Model Bill)	Ministry of Finance, Government of Nepal
2	Province and Local Appropriation Act (Model Bill)	
3	Province and Local Consolidated Fund Operation Act (Model Bill)	
4	Province and Local Financial Procedure Law (Model)	
5	Province and Local Tax and Non-Tax Revenue Act (Model)	
6	Province and Local Fiscal Management Act (Model)	
7	Province and Local Budget Formulation Guidelines (Model)	
8	Business Tax procedure (2019) (Model)	Ministry of Federal Affairs and General Administration, Government of Nepal
9	Revenue Improvement Action Plan (2019) (Model)	
10	House Land Rental Income Tax Procedure (2019) (Model)	
11	Public Procurement Regulation (2018) (Model)	
12	Tax and Non-Tax Revenue related procedure (2017) (Model)	
13	Integrated Property Tax Procedure (2017) (Model)	
14	Local Finance Act (Bill) (2017) (Model)	
15	Local Appropriation Act Bill (2017) (Model)	
16	Local Level Annual Budget Guideline (2017) (Model)	
17	Financial Procedure Regulation and Management Rule (2017) (Model)	
18	Province Fiscal Management Act (2017) (Model)	Ministry of Law, Justice and Parliamentary Affairs, Government of Nepal
19	Province Tax and Non-Tax Revenue Act (2017) (Model)	
20	Province Finance Act (2017) (Model)	
21	Province Emergency (AkasmikKosh) Fund Operation and Management Act (2018) (Model)	
22	Province Financial Procedure (Regulation and Management) Law (Model)	

Appendix 10: Provincial Grants Provided to Local Government FY2018–FY2021 (NRs million)

S. No	Details/FYs	2018 Budget	2018 Actual	2019 Budget	2019 Actual	2020 Budget	2020 Actual	2021 Budget	2021 Actual
Province 1									
1	Fiscal Equalization				499.99	999.99	999.99	999.99	NA
2	Conditional				3,143.08	2,268.70	2,971.30	619.70	NA
3	Complementary	Budget is not segregated				1,125.00	1,411.50	1,407.00	NA
4	Special					399.60	441.71	–	NA
	Total	–	–	3,000.00	3,643.07	4,793.29	5,824.50	3,026.69	NA
Province 2									
1	Fiscal Equalization				400.00	999.98	–	–	NA
2	Conditional				132.80	1,587.58	167.00	181.44	NA
3	Complementary		NA			630.25	–	–	NA
4	Special					342.15	–	82.00	NA
	Total	–	–	–	532.80	3,559.96	167.00	263.44	NA
Bagmati Province									
1	Fiscal Equalization				–		1,248.80	1,250.00	NA
2	Conditional			3,742.40	–	278.15	1,897.07	3,064.55	NA
3	Complementary			880.60	–		1,217.80	2,631.60	NA
4	Special			650.00	–		197.58	297.00	NA
	Total	–	–	5,273.00	–	278.15	4,561.25	7,243.15	NA
Gandaki Province									
1	Fiscal Equalization			1,000.00	1,000.00	976.95	,139.28	1,046.26	NA
2	Conditional					201.40	290.81	303.69	NA
3	Complementary			100.00	18.95	196.78	300.03	590.01	NA
4	Special			100.00	32.89	43.85	64.34	177.85	NA
	Total	–	–	1,200.00	1,051.84	1,418.98	1,794.46	2,117.81	NA

Continued on next page

Appendix 10   Continued

S. No	Details/FYs	2018 Budget	2018 Actual	2019 Budget	2019 Actual	2020 Budget	2020 Actual	2021 Budget	2021 Actual
Lumbini Province									
1	Fiscal Equalization			500.00	500.00	500.00	499.99	600.00	NA
2	Conditional			1,000.00	994.12	2,569.56	1,343.26	2,040.55	NA
3	Complementary			–	358.21	1,500.00	1,424.71	1,512.31	NA
4	Special			–	9.80	1,000.00	964.35	1,018.46	NA
	Total	–	–	1,500.00	1,862.13	5,569.56	4,232.31	5,171.32	NA
Karnali Province									
1	Fiscal Equalization			–	–	–	800.00	795.78	NA
2	Conditional			–	–	699.96	527.80	471.00	NA
3	Complementary			–	765.18	650.00	394.02	277.00	NA
4	Special			–	–	150.00	181.91	795.50	NA
	Total	–	–	–	765.18	1,499.96	1,903.73	2,339.28	NA
Sudurpashchim Province									
1	Fiscal Equalization			620.00	620.00	622.17	621.17	629.23	NA
2	Conditional			32.90	30.30	1,750.00	1,017.83	541.18	NA
3	Complementary			1,005.67	134.78	1,084.10	670.93	933.76	NA
4	Special			500.00	239.55	700.00	456.19	474.75	NA
	Total	–	–	2,158.57	1,024.63	4,156.27	2,766.12	2,578.92	NA